LITTLE MAN COMPUTER PROGRAMMING FOR THE PERPLEXED

- FROM THE GROUND UP

UNDERSTANDING THE LITTLE MAN COMPUTER AND LEARNING HOW TO DESIGN, WRITE AND UNDERSTAND LITTLE MAN COMPUTER PROGRAMS.

LEARN WHAT YOU NEED TO KNOW TO PASS LITTLE MAN COMPUTER BASED PROJECTS, PROGRAMMING ASSIGNMENTS, AND BE ABLE TO ANSWER LITTLE MAN COMPUTER EXAM QUESTIONS, OR HOW TO BETTER USE THE LITTLE MAN COMPUTER IN YOUR COMPUTER SCIENCE TEACHING PRACTICE.

ISBN 978-0-9935315-2-1

Published by:
The Internet Technical Bookshop
awe@itbs.co.uk
www.itbs.co.uk

INTRODUCTION

Governments all over the world are actively developing and enhancing computing and IT education across a very wide age range ranging from pre-school all the way through to technical training college level, university level and beyond. Studying computing and IT is a lifelong process. Technology is changing and evolving at an ever increasing pace. Economic, industrial and social development is becoming ever more closely tied in with mastering and exploiting developments in computing and IT.

Designing , Developing and Deploying (D3) a computing and IT curriculum is a complex task. As well as developing the curriculum itself there is, in its early stages (i.e. now) the challenging task of supporting and nurturing those who will be teaching in this area. This is especially true of non-specialists who will form the majority of those teaching computing to younger children.

I first came across the Little Man Computer when writing and teaching a first year introduction to computing course at UMUC (University of Maryland University College) , a distance learning college similar to the Open University in the UK. The set book for this course was Irv Englander's "The Architecture of Computer Hardware and Systems Software: An Information Technology Approach". The students on this course mostly came from those working for local and federal US Government agencies as well as those from the armed forces. Mostly they came from backgrounds where attendance at an "Ivy League University" was beyond their wildest dreams because of the great costs involved in studying at such institutions. It was a joy and a privilege to work with these students many of whom were quite outstanding and able.

This, "little book", is written in the hope that it will be of help to as many students, parents, home educators and teachers as possible. Making sense of computer instruction sets and writing code in assembler is far from easy. These days assembly language programming is taught less and less, even though it does have a role to play in the development of embedded systems such as the ever increasing number of such systems being developed as "things" for the "Internet of Things".

Writing assembly language programs requires being able to formulate and structure these problems at a higher level, before coming up with the final assembly language code. Thus simply learning about the Little Man Computer and "his" inner workings is not enough. It is also necessary to think about (and to teach thinking about) how the problem is to be tackled, starting off with thinking about a problem at a high level and then gradually breaking it down into a more detailed design using techniques such as hierarchical decomposition, pseudo code and flow charting. These topics will be explored in this book.

Obviously teachers and instructors will have to adapt the various topics covered in this book to the needs of their students, and students using this book will need to focus on those topics that they are having problems with.

I hope that this book will be of use to both A Level and College/University Undergraduate Level teachers as well as to students struggling with "the mysteries of Little Man Computer (LMC) assembly language programming.

My other hope is that this book will also serve as a "stepping stone" to real world assembly language programming.

Follow on books in this series of books will include:

- Atmel AVR 8 Assembly Language Programming.
- 8051 Assembly Language Programming.
- ARM Cortex M0, M3 and M4 Assembly Language Programming.
- PIC10, PIC12, PIC16 and PIC18 Assembler Language Programming.
- PIC24 and dsPIC Assembler Language Programming.
- PIC32 MIPS Assembly Languge Programming.

TABLE OF CONTENTS

CHAPTER 1
The Mysterious Inner Workings of Computers

1.1. Computers and What they do

These days computers come in all shapes and sizes. Mobile phones, laptops, electricity meters, traffic light controllers, electronic jewellery are all examples of computers. So what is a computer ?

Answer - a computer is something (a device) that computes. This sounds like a circular definition, but it isn't. To compute at its simplest is to calculate. The earliest computers were simply glorified calculators. However they could do calculations awfully fast. Initially they were very expensive and very large. But with the invention of transistors and then integrated circuits they became smaller and cheaper.

Calculations with numbers are simply the results of doing things with numbers. The technical way of describing this is to say "performing operations on numbers". A number can be represented using symbols. When first learning arithmetic we use strings (words) made up of decimal numbers to represent actual numbers. The kinds of things we can do with numbers are

- Adding a number to another number.
- Subtracting a number from a number.
- Multiplying a number by a number.
- Dividing a number by a number.

Zero is, at first, a strange number, as is the idea of a negative number. Fractions and fractional numbers are even more tricky. The little man computer can recognise when a subtraction of one number from another results in a negative value. It does not, however, allow negative numbers to be entered into it. The little man computer , also , does not do fractions or fractional arithmetic.

Numbers are a representation of something. It is up to us how to associate a particular number with some particular meaning. In fact, numbers can also be used to represent other things, providing we know that the number we are looking at is being used to represent something. A number can be used to represent a letter of the alphabet, and different numbers can be used to represent lowercase letters and uppercase letters. If each letter is represented by a particular number and no two different letters can have the same number then numbers can be used to manipulate letters and words. All that is required is that the context in which a number is used and interpreted is known at the time it is being used.

Computers, also, need to be able to remember things. For example we may want to enter a list of numbers and then ask the computer to add those numbers up, or we may want the computer to find the largest or smallest number in the list, or whether a particular number is present in the list.

Computers can only do what they are told to do. Simple computers are very obedient and do not have any imagination of their own. They cannot "read your mind" or cope with vague instructions such as, for example, "save that value somewhere". You have to tell the computer exactly where to save a value, or where to fetch a value from. You tell a computer what to do by providing it with a list of instructions. Most computers have a relatively small number of basic instructions that they understand. However, if the instructions are chosen carefully when designing the computer they can be used to produce programs that can performs all kinds of useful calculations. Devising a good set of instructions for a computer is not as easy as you might assume.

Inside a computer the instructions are represented as numbers. The computer needs to know when it looks at a value somewhere in its memory whether that value represents an instruction, or a number or a letter, or even a some other location in its memory.

1.2 Operations and Operands and the workings of the Little Man Computer :

A computer processes instructions. When a computer is running it knows the location of the next instruction it is to fetch and execute. This location address (value), in most computer processors, is held in a special register (location) called the program counter.

Normally, after a given instruction has been executed the program counter is moved on to the location of the next instruction which is at the address that follows the instruction it has just executed. However, some instructions can alter the value of the program counter. These kinds of instructions are called "branching" instructions because they "branch off" to a different location. They are very important in the construction of computer programs and the Little Man Computer must handle them properly.

The answer to the question "What is an instruction ?" is not too easy and not too difficult. In "computing speak" an instruction consists of an OPERATION and zero or more OPERANDS.

You can think of an OPERATION as an instruction to "DO THIS" and you can think of the OPERANDS as the things you are to use when "DOING THIS".

You can examine spoken instructions and try to identify the OPERATION and the OPERANDS.

As an example in the sentence "Kick the ball"

What is the OPERATION ?

What is the OPERAND ?

I hope that you thought that the OPERATION is KICK and that the OPERAND is BALL.

Imagine a world of books and shelves and a table in which a shelf can only, ever, have at most one book on it, and a table can only ever have at most one book on it.

In the sentence "Put the book on the top shelf" we could think of the operation as PUT and the two operands as BOOK and TOP_SHELF. The interesting thing here is that TOP_SHELF denotes a location. Locations in a computer correspond to locations in memory. A location in memory is called an ADDRESS. Putting something into a memory location is referred to as WRITING TO MEMORY.

Similarly , in a sentence such as "Take the book from the top shelf and put it on the table" we can think of the operation as TAKE_AND_PUT and the operands as TOP_SHELF and TABLE. This is a little tricky and depends on the fact that in our special world we only have books, shelves and a table. A TAKE_AND_PUT operation corresponds to READING FROM MEMORY.

The world of the LITTLE MAN COMPUTER is not that different from the world of BOOKS, SHELVES and a TABLE. In the world of the LITTLE MAN COMPUTER

- There is a Mailroom in which a Little Man does his work.
- Inside the Mailroom
- There is a rack of numbered mailboxes each of which can hold a single instruction written on a piece of paper
- There is a calculator which is used by the Little Man inside the Computer to do calculations asked for by a given instruction.
- There is a counter which displays the location of the next instruction to process (i.e. which mailbox to go to to get the slip of paper with the instruction written on it).
- This counter has a reset button that can be operated from outside the mail room and which sets the counter back to 0.
- Also, there is a button which can be pressed to move the counter to the next location value
- The mailroom also has an In Basket which can be used for entering instructions and an Out Basket into which results can be placed.

In his introductory book on computers and information technology [4] Irv Englanded sketched out the world of the Little Man Computer which he envisaged as something like the following. The drawing describing the original Little Man Computer is very simple, but does the job.

Fig 1.1. Outline of the Architecture of a Little Man Computer

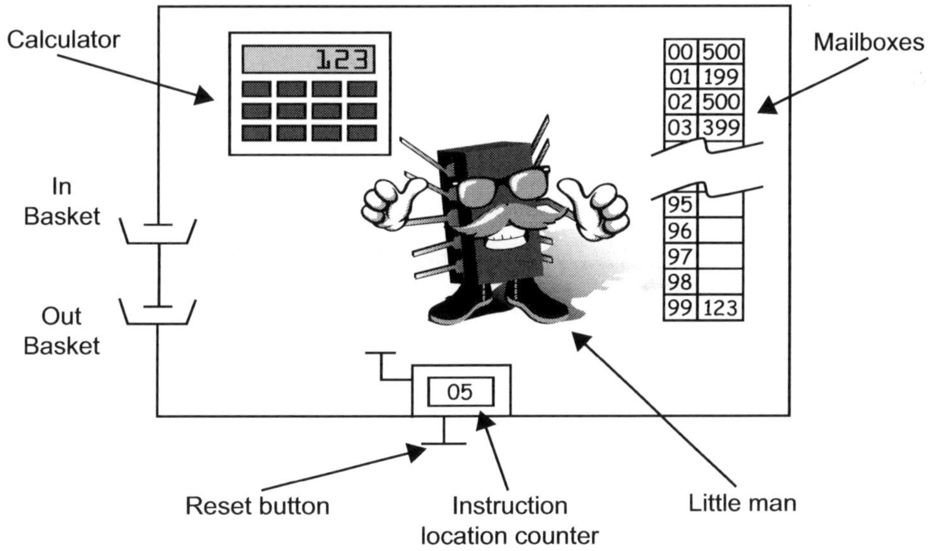

Some important details regarding the Little Man Computer

When designing a computer processor and associated peripherals such as input and output devices e.g. printers and keyboards questions arise such as

- How complex should each instruction be ?
- How many instructions should be present in the instruction set ?
- How many mailboxes should there be ?
- Remember that the more mailboxes there are the bigger the size of a mailbox address, think of a street of houses - the longer the street the greater the number of house numbers required.
- How many instructions can a mailbox contain ?
    - The answer is exactly one instruction.
- What is the calculator capable of calculating ?
    - On simple systems calculations involve only small non fractional numbers.
- The LMC Calculator can be used to enter numbers and to store those numbers whilst they are needed for some calculation.
- The LMC Calculator display can only display three digits as the LMC Computer uses exactly three digits to represent instructions or data values.
- The LMC calculator cannot do calculations involving negative numbers.
- What is the nature of the Instruction Location Counter
    - It can be thought of as a hand counter used to e.g. count the passengers on a plane, similar to e.g. the one shown in Fig 1.2.
    - Clicking the hand counter once simply increments the counter value (i.e. adds one to it).
    - The hand counter also has a set of thumbwheels to change the value in the counter directly when necessary.
    - There is also a reset button - which can be accessed from outside the Mailroom, and which resets the counter value to zero.
- How do you interact with the Little Man Computer
    - The only mechanisms for interacting with the Little Man Computer are via the In Basket and the Out Basket.
    - A user, who is not allowed into the Mailroom, can only place little slips of paper into the In Basket.
    - Only one slip of paper can be placed into the In Basket at a time
    - The only thing that can be written on that slip of paper is a three digit number.
    - The only way a user can receive output from the Little Man Computer is when the Little Man Computer writes a three digit number on a slip of paper and puts it in the Out Basket.
- Thus, the only communications between the Little Man Computer and the outside world are
    - Via three digit numbers
    - By pressing the Reset Button of the Instruction Location Counter.
- What of the Little Man that drives the Little Man Computer
    - His is a world in which all instructions are written as three digit numbers
    - He knows how to interpret these instructions
    - He cannot demonstrate any initiative on his own.

This all sounds very contrived but such designs are a consequence of the fact that computers are implemented out of electronic and, sometimes, mechanical mechanisms.

Fig 1.2 A Mini Hand Tally Counter

In the Mini Hand Tally Counter shown, clicking the button on top moves (increments) the counter value by 1. The thumbwheel on the right can be used to set the counter value to an chosen value. The little man computer counter can only display two digits, whereas the one shown here can display four digits.

1.3 The Instructions the Man in the Little Man Computer Understands

The instructions used by the Little Man Computer are exactly three digits long.

- The first digit is the OPERATION part of the instruction and encodes the operation to be performed.
- The OPERATION code is often abbreviated to op code.
- The remaining two digits are the OPERAND and, in the world of the Little Man Computer, represent a mailbox address.

Fig 1.3 The Structure of a Little Man Computer Instruction.

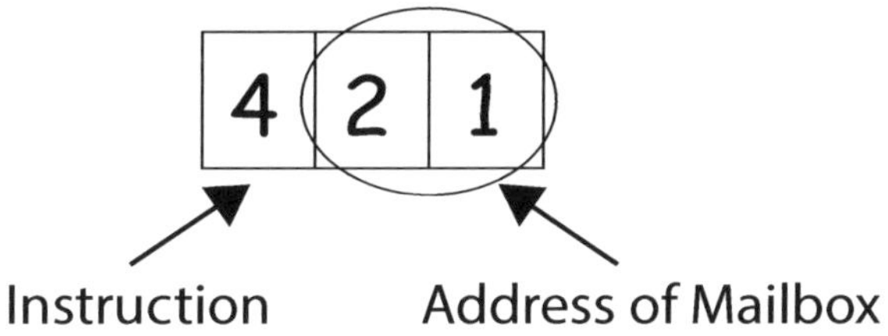

The little man in the Little Man Computer can

- Read the three digit number displayed by the calculator and copy it onto a slip of paper for storing in a mailbox.
- Read the instruction location counter.
- Manipulate the instruction location counter.

The instructions the Little Man Computer uses can be split into two groups

- Basic instructions - such as STORE, ADD, INPUT
- Extended instructions - used to make either unconditional, or conditional branching decisions e.g.
    - BRANCH ON POSITIVE

1.3.1 The Core LMC Instructions.

There are four kinds of core instruction

- Instructions used to move data from one part of the LMC to another - LOAD and STORE instructions
- Instructions used to do simple arithmetic - ADD and SUBTRACT
- Instructions used for input and output - INPUT and OUTPUT
- An instruction to stop the LMC , HALT, sometimes referred to as the "COFFEE BREAK" instruction.

In this section we will go through these instructions in turn and then use them to implement a very small program that adds two numbers together.

1.3.1.1 The Data Moving Instructions

LOAD : The opcode for this instruction is 5 and the operand is an address

The instruction works in the following manner.

- The Little Man goes to the mailbox address given by the operand.
- He reads the three digit number he finds in that location.
- The original slip of paper stays where it is in the mailbox.
- He goes to the calculator and enters that number into the calculator - which now becomes the new number displayed by the calculator.

STORE : The opcode for this instruction is 3 and the operand is an address

This instruction is the converse of the LOAD instruction and works in the following manner.

- The Little Man goes to the calculator and reads the number it is displaying.
- He writes that number on a slip of paper.
- The number temporarily stored in the calculator and being displayed by the calculator does not change.
- He goes to the mailbox with the address given on the instruction and puts the slip of paper in that mailbox, removing the previous slip of paper if there was one there.

1.3.1.2 The Arithmetic Instructions

ADD : The opcode for this instruction is 1 and the operand is an address

The instruction works in the following manner.

- The Little Man goes to the mailbox address given by the operand.
- He reads the three digit number he finds in that location.
- The original slip of paper stays where it is in the mailbox.
- He goes to the calculator and adds that number to the number which is already stored in the calculator
- The result of the addition becomes the new number displayed by the calculator.

SUBTRACT : The opcode for this instruction is 2 and the operand is an address
The instruction works in the following manner.

- The Little Man goes to the mailbox address given by the operand.
- He reads the three digit number he finds in that location.
- The original slip of paper stays where it is in the mailbox.
- He goes to the calculator and subtracts that number from the number which is already stored in the calculator
- The result of the subtraction becomes the new number displayed by the calculator.
- The LMC model does not have any way of representing and saving negative numbers to a mailbox, or of retrieving negative numbers from the mailbox.
- The calculator can, however, hold a negative result and has a minus flag to indicate that the result was negative.
- It will perform arithmetic involving negative numbers correctly.
- There is no mechanism for handling negative numbers outside of the calculator.

1.3.1.3 The Input and Output Instructions

INPUT : The opcode for this instruction is 9 and the operand has an address value of 01

The instruction works in the following manner.

- The Little Man goes to the In Basket.
- He reads the three digit number he finds on the slip of paper in the In Basket.
- He disposes of the slip of paper he took from the In Basket.
- He goes to the calculator and enters that number into the calculator - which now becomes the new number displayed by the calculator.
- An input instruction will always be 901.
- Note: The address 01 is a "dummy" address.

STORE : The opcode for this instruction is 9 and the operand has an address value of 02

This instruction works in the following manner

- The Little Man goes to the calculator and writes down the number displayed by the calculator on a slip of paper.
- He then goes to the Out Basket and puts the slip of paper into the basket, from where it can be retrieved by the user, who, is , of course, outside of the mailroom and is not allowed to witness the internal steps traced out by the Little Man.
- Note that the number being displayed, which is the number being temporarily stored in the calculator is not changed.
- An output instruction will always be 902.

1.3.1.4 The HALT instruction

HALT / STOP : The opcode for this instruction is 0.

- The address part of the instruction is ignored
- The effect of the instruction is for the Little Man to stop trying to execute any further instructions.
- In effect we can think of this as an instruction that allows the Little Man to have a rest, in effect to have a "COFFEE BREAK".

1.4 How Does the Little Man Execute a Program, and how can you make sense of a Little Man Computer Program ?

Later on I will show you how to write instructions to enter a program into the Little Man Computer.

Suppose, for now, that a set of instructions has been deposited in the various mailboxes in the LMC Mailroom, and that the Program Counter has been set to 00, by the program user by pressing the Reset Button, which, as you know, is located outside the Mailroom, and is therefore accessible.

When the program counter is set to zero, the Little Man, who even while resting was keeping an eye on the program counter, knows that he must go to the mailbox with address 00 and fetch the instruction at that address, and keep on fetching and processing instructions till he encounters the HALT instruction, at which point he can "take another break".

Table 1.1 shows a listing of our little program.

Table 1.1 A Small Example Program

Mailbox Address	Instruction
00	901
01	399
02	901
03	199
04	902
05	0
99	

Looking at this list of numbers you might well get a sinking feeling "how will I ever learn how to write Little Man Computer programs ?" . The early programmers faced exactly the same difficulties, except all the instructions were in binary and had to be entered either by toggling switches, or by reading a paper tape, or by reading punched cards which had to be prepared.

Fig 1.4 A PDP 8 Computer showing toggle switches.

Fig 1.5 Paper Tape Reader Used for PDP 8 Minicomputers

The secret to writing computer programs is to write them in a language that is more readable, and then to write a program that can translate a program written in such a readable language into machine code. The earliest languages developed for just this purpose were called Assembler languages. Instead of machine code mnemonics for the operands and operations were invented, and labels for naming various mailbox (memory) locations were used to make the code easier to follow.

The descriptions of the various Little Man Computer instructions provide suitable mnemonics for the various operations the Little Man Computer can perform.

If we take the above little program and add a third column in which we write descriptions of the instructions the code should be easier to follow, We are, in effect , using a the little language to describe our program. Our descriptions are the foundations for a little language - an Assembly language, because the machine instructions can be "Assembled" from it. If we design our Assembly language grammar, and symbols / words carefully we can implement an Assembler program that translates our program written in assembler into machine instructions. Reading a program written in assembler is much easier, for most people, than reading machine code directly.

Table 1.2 Small Example Program with Description of Each Instruction

Mailbox Address	Instruction	Instruction Description
00	901	INPUT ; First number
01	399	STORE 99 ; Store at the DATA address
02	901	INPUT ; Second number
03	199	ADD DATA ; Add value stored in the DATA address (the first number entered) to the value stored in the calculator (the second number entered)
04	902	OUTPUT ; Output the RESULT
05	0	HALT
99		; DATA

Looking at the above table you should be able to make out that this little program adds two numbers entered by the user and outputs (returns) the sum of those two numbers.

1.5 Extended Little Man Computer Instructions for Branching to New Locations

All computer programs are based on the following instruction processing abilities

- SEQUENCE - executing one instruction after another sequentially
- ITERATION - executing a group of instructions in a cycle repeatedly for some specified number of repetitions, or , if needs be forever.
- BRANCHING - branching to a different part of the code

Structured programming depends to a large extent on being to break up a problem into simpler pieces of code that provide the required functionality implemented in code using these mechanisms.

The Little Man Computer provides only very basic branching mechanisms. Real computers support all these mechanisms, but, in addition provide the ability to call functions, and the ability to handle interrupts generated by peripherals.

Interrupts are special and most code written in languages such as C or BASIC or Python has nothing directly to do with interrupts. However interrupts are important when writing low level code. When an interrupt happens the computer automatically finishes of the instruction it was executing, saves information about the context in which that instruction was being executed as well as the address of the next instruction that program is to execute, so that it can be restored later, and then branches to the address where the code that deals with that interrupt is located. At the end of the interrupt the context is restored and the program counter is set to the next instruction that would have been executed had the interrupt not occurred. We will cover implementing and calling functions and, interrupt handling in a follow-on book where our knowledge of Little Man Computer programming is extended further and applied to a real world small microcontroller, a Microchip PIC16 microcontroller.

1.5.1 Little Man Computer Branching Instructions

BRANCH UNCONDITIONALLY (BR) : The opcode for this instruction is 6

The instruction works in the following manner.

- The Little Man goes to the instruction counter (program counter) and actually changes the counter value to the address given by the operand part of the instruction.
- He does this by using the thumbwheels on the hand counter.
- The instruction at that address is the next instruction that the Little Man will execute.
- Note: The Little Man expects to find an instruction at the address specified by the operand. It is up to the programmer to ensure that there is indeed a valid instruction at that address.

BRANCH ON ZERO (BRZ) : The opcode for this instruction is 7

The instruction works in the following manner.

- The Little Man goes to the calculator and looks at the number being shown by the calculator.
- If the value being shown by the calculator is zero, the Little Man goes to the instruction counter (program counter) and actually changes the counter value to the address given by the operand part of the instruction.
- He does this by using the thumbwheels on the hand counter.
- The instruction at that address is the next instruction that the Little Man will execute.
- Note: The Little Man expects to find an instruction at the address specified by the operand. It is up to the programmer to ensure that there is indeed a valid instruction at that address.
- If the value being shown by the calculator is not zero then the Little Man simply executes the next instruction.

BRANCH ON POSITIVE (BRP) : The opcode for this instruction is 8

The instruction works in the following manner.

- The Little Man goes to the calculator and looks at the number being shown by the calculator.
- If the value being shown by the calculator is a positive number, the Little Man goes to the instruction counter (program counter) and actually changes the counter value to the address given by the operand part of the instruction.
- He does this by using the thumbwheels on the hand counter.
- The instruction at that address is the next instruction that the Little Man will execute.
- Note: The Little Man expects to find an instruction at the address specified by the operand. It is up to the programmer to ensure that there is indeed a valid instruction at that address.
- If the value being shown by the calculator is not a positive number then the Little Man simply executes the next instruction.

1.5.2 Example of A Little Man Computer Program That Uses Branching Instructions.

In this little program the user inputs two numbers. The program outputs the greater of these two numbers

Table 1.3 A Program which Reads Two Numbers and Outputs the Larger Number

Mailbox Address	Instruction	Instruction Description
00	901	INPUT ; First number
01	309	STORE 9 ; Store at address 9
02	901	INPUT ; Second number
03	310	STORE 10; Store at address 10
04	209	SUB 9 ; Subtract the first number entered (it was stored at address 9) from the second number entered (which is still in the calculator)
05	808	BRP 07 ; If the result is positive (the first number entered is smaller than the second number entered)
06	509	LOAD 9; Load the first number entered into the calculator
07	902	OUTPUT; Output the number currently stored in the calculator.
08	000	HALT ; Terminate program.
09	000	; Location for the first number. It is initialised to 000 so that if the program gets here thinking it contains an instruction it will HALT
10	000	; Location for the second number. It is initialised to 000 so that if the program gets here thinking it contains an instruction it will HALT

This program illustrates several interesting aspects of computer programming using an architecture where code and data are stored in the same mailboxes (Memory). Such an architecture is called a Von Neuman architecture (after its inventor John von Neuman, one of the founders of modern computing). It is also sometimes called the Princeton architecture because von Neuman worked at Princeton. The rival architecture, called the Harvard architecture, (Harvard and Princeton are great rivals) places code in one memory space and data in a different memory space.

In the case of the Von Neuman architecture it is necessary to know whether a particular entry in a mailbox is an instruction, or is data. A common approach is to use the top part of memory for instructions (code) and the bottom part of memory for data. It is up to the programmer to know where the boundary between the code memory and the data memory areas lies.

1.6 Entering a Program Into the Little Man Computer

You may have been wondering as to how a program gets into the Little Man Computer. Instructions are three digit quantities and the biggest numbers the Little Man Computer can handle are two digit numbers.

What is needed is some mechanism for getting the Little Man to enter an instruction into the computer. An instruction consists of an OPCODE followed by two digits, i.e. it occupies three digits. An instruction to load an instruction would occupy four digits. In real world computers such problems are sometimes dealt with by having instructions that actually take up two or three instruction slots.

In the case of the Little Man Computer there are various possible strategies that might be devised. This problem is not really discussed much in connection with the Little Man Computer. For teaching purposes "the program somehow gets into the computer". However if we had to construct a program to actually enter a program into the Little Man Computer we would need to have an instruction that would load an instruction into a particular address.

One way of doing this might be the following.

- Note that opcode 4 is currently not used.
- We could devise (invent) an instruction 4xx that means that the next slip of paper will have an instruction on it and that xx is the mailbox address into which that instruction is to be placed,
- When the Little Man encounters a 4xx instruction he will
- Note the mailbox address on the first slip of paper
- Pick up the second slip of paper and enter that instruction into the mailbox at the address he has noted down.

As you can see this whole area of devising instruction sets is potentially quite a complicated subject.

Fortunately the Little Man Computer simulations we will be using separate the program entry stage from the program running phase. The program is written in an assembly language. It is then assembled to generate the machine code, and the machine code is then loaded into the Little Man Computer. Setting the program counter to zero starts off the program. In addition we can run the program to completion, or step through the program one instruction at a time.

Exercises

1. Create a little world of your own and invent things that can be done in that world and the kinds of instructions needed to tell someone what is to be done.

For each instruction work out what is the OPERATION and what are the OPERANDs.

2. Envisage the world of the Little Man Computer and create a model of it as a drawing, or a construction out of e.g Lego or even Plasticine. [Note: If you search the internet you will actually discover examples projects doing such things]

3. Do some research on the internet and see if you can come up with answers to the following questions:

   - How much memory did a PDP 8 computer have, typically ?
   - How much did a PDP 8 Computer cost ?
   - Are there any places where a vintage PDP 8 computer has been restored into a condition where it can run computer programs ?
   - What did the instruction set of a PDP 8 computer look like ?

4. Choose one of the core Little Man Computer Instructions and describe how it works as a sequence of cartoon frames. You can add speech bubbles to show "what the Little Man is thinking".

CHAPTER 2
Little Man Computer Assembly Language Programming

Various implementations of Little Man Computer simulations and their associated assemblers have been devised over the years since the Little Man Computer was first introduced. Here, we will use the simulation and assembler developed by Peter Higginson. This has a web browser based interface. The URL for getting hold of Peter's version of the Little Man Computer is http://peterhigginson.co.uk/LMC/ . The actual implementation is written in Java Script and the script itself can be downloaded and studied if you are curious.

2.1 The Higginson Little Man Computer

The Higginson Little Man Computer simulator looks like this

Fig 2.1 The Higginson Little Man Computer Simulator Interface

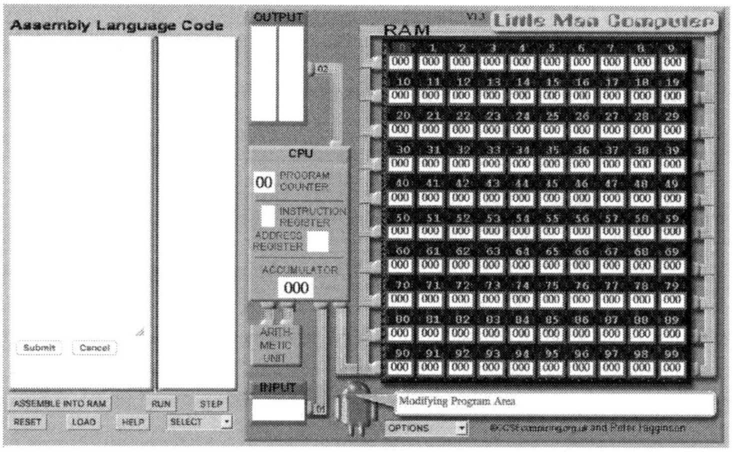

Looking at this simulator interface you should be able to locate the following elements:

100 Memory locations (numbered 0 to 99).

- An Arithmetic Unit which performs the calculations.
- An Accumulator which stores the result of the last operation or calculation.
- A Program Counter used to store the memory address of the next instruction to execute.
- An Instruction Register which holds the top digit (the opcode digit) of the instruction read from memory.
- An Address Register which holds the bottom two digits (the operand) of the instruction read from memory.

- An Input tray into which a number can be typed when required.
- An Output area where output is printed.

2.2. The Higginson Little Man Computer Assembler - An Overview

The assembler mnemonics for the Higginson Little Man Computer are summarised in the following table.

Code	Name	Description
0	HLT	Stop (Little Man has a rest).
1	ADD	Add the contents of the memory address to the Accumulator
2	SUB	Subtract the contents of the memory address from the Accumulator
3	STA or STO	Store the value in the Accumulator in the memory address given.
4		This code is unused and attempting to use it gives an error.
5	LDA	Load the Accumulator with the contents of the memory address given
6	BRA	Branch - use the address given as the address of the next instruction
7	BRZ	Branch to the address given if the Accumulator is zero
8	BRP	Branch to the address given if the Accumulator is zero or positive
9	INP or OUT	Input or Output. Take from Input if address is 1, copy to Output if address is 2.
9	OTC	Output accumulator as a character if address is 22. (Nonstandard instruction)

In this implementation it is possible to output both numbers (OUT) and characters (OTC). On a real computer there would , most likely, only be an OTC instruction and the program would have to convert numbers to characters before printing. The same considerations hold for input , however, this simulation provides INP as a simple means for inputting numbers.

The Higginson Little Man Computer simulation comes with a built in assembler. The assembler permits addresses to be associated with names (labels).

Any word that is not a recognisable instruction is assumed to be a label. If the label occurs before an instruction or before a DAT then it is considered as defining an address.

If the label occurs after the instruction (operation) or after a DAT then the address associated with that label is substituted for the label.

There are two text areas to the left of the LMC. The leftmost area is an assembler editor area (window) where assembler can be typed in. The area to the right of it displays the machine code generated by the assembler.

In this assembler any line beginning with a // is a comment. Comment lines are ignored by the assembler. It is generally considered good practice to comment code, especially tricky bits of code, so that the code is easier to follow and understand.

Comments can also be put after instructions. The assembler looks only for an optional initial label, an instruction code and an address for the instruction when it is processing a line that is not a comment line. Anything after the address (operand) is ignored, and, hence is treated as comment.

Where an address is omitted a default address of 0 will , normally, be used. However, where an address is omitted and a comment added an error will result.

This particular assembler is case insensitive and instructions can be entered in lower case, upper case or a mixture of both, and these will be identified in a case insensitive way i.e. sub and SUB refer to the same instruction. In the case of labels the matching is case sensitive and so LOOP and loop used as labels are different labels. Differentiating labels using case (e.g. LOOP and loop) is generally frowned upon as it can lead to accidental errors in the code.

Probably the easiest way of gaining familiarity with the Little Man Computer is to work though the example programs that are supplied with it. The list of example programs can be displayed by clicking on the SELECT dropown menu button.

Fig 2.2. Higginson Little Man Computer Example Programs

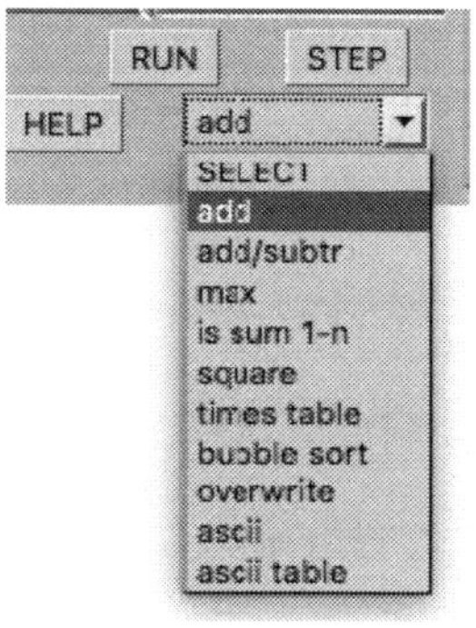

Over the course of the remainder of this book the plan is to work carefully through most of these examples so as to "suck out" useful design and programming patterns, and, also to add some more examples that extend these examples. In addition we will consider how to tackle the kinds of "practical and experiential" projects and assignments that you will come across in GCSE and A Level courses in the UK, in the International Baccalaureate courses abroad, and also in high school and undergraduate "introduction to computing" courses.

2.3 Basic Maths Programs on the Little Man Computer.

The Little Man Computer is very limited in the mathematical operations it supports. However these basic operations can be used to implement other operations. Given the ability to add and subtract it is possible to implement more complex mathematical operations such as multiplication and division. We will explore more complex programs in the next chapter where we introduce structured programming techniques based on the use of pseudocode and flowcharts.

2.3.1 Basic Addition

This is one of the most basic Little Man Computer programs it is possible to implement, namely, to have a user input two numbers and to then output the sum of those two numbers. There is already a simple demonstration program provided with the simulator we are using that does this. The program, quite unsurprisingly is called add.

Selecting add results in both the assembler and machine code being displayed in the corresponding text windows, and the assembled program being loaded into the Little Man Computer.

Fig 2.3 The "add" Program - Assembly code and Entries in Mailboxes once the program has been loaded into the Little Man Computer

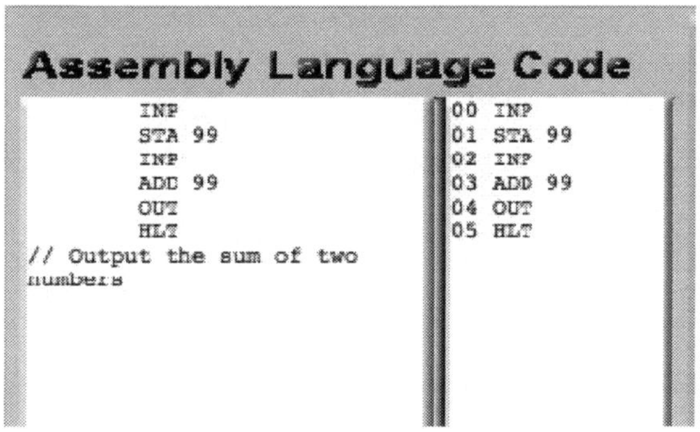

Table 2.1 'add' Program Showing Mailbox contents with descriptions

Mailbox Address	Instruction	Instruction in Assembler	Description
00	901	INP	Input first number
01	399	STA 99	Store it at address 99
02	901	INP	Input second number
03	199	ADD 99	Add number stored at address 99 to it
04	902	OUT	Output the result
05	000	HLT	Halt the program

We are now in a position to, intelligently, step through the code. We do this by pressing the step button to get the Little Man to move on to the next instruction. If the Little Man is waiting for some input he will not be able to move on till we have provided him with some suitable input.

If we press the STEP button moving red and blue dots will trace the path taken by data and instructions between the various components of the Little Man Computer such as the Input and Output Baskets, the various parts of the CPU (Instruction Counter, Instruction , Address and Accumulator). For an input the Input basket will end up having a flashing cursor in it. This is a hint for us to enter a number, 10 say. We indicate that we have entered a number by pressing the enter key after we have typed in the digits for that number. At this point a blue dot traces the path taken by the Little Man and the entry of the number into the accumulator (which holds the value being stored temporarily in the calculator and displays it). Also the mailbox number of the mailbox containing the next instruction to execute is highlighted in red. On pressing STEP again the path taken to save the number entered into mailbox with address 99 is shown. Also, when running the siimulation, notice the explanatory messages being displayed by the Little Man "Robot Icon" , and notice that the mailbox address of the mailbox containing the next instruction is now highlighted in red.

Fig 2.4 State of the Little Man Computer after the first number has been entered and stored at memory address 99

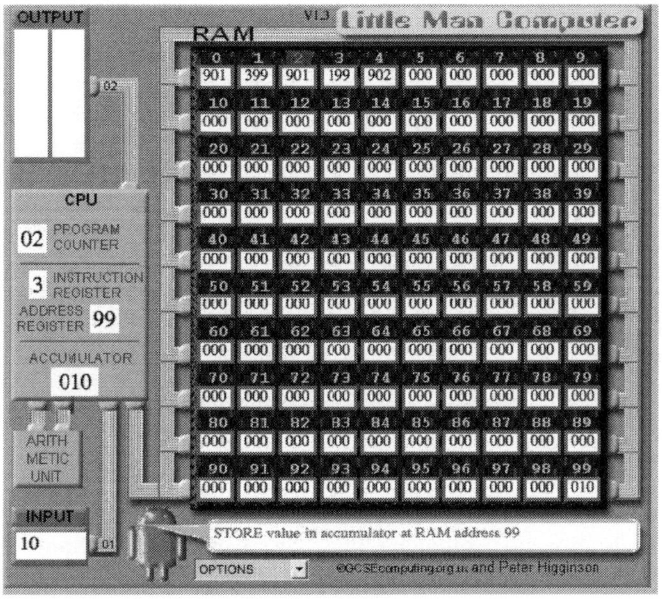

Continue stepping through the program, entering the second number when prompted to do so.

At each stage check the values in the CPU

- Does the program counter show the correct value ?
- Do the intruction register and the address register reflect the instruction that has just been executed ?
- Is the value displayed in the accumulator what you would expect ?

If all went well and you entered 10 as the first number and 11 as the second number then finally the output displayed in the output box should be 21.

So far so good. However, we have been sensible about the numbers we have been entering.

Try out the following experiments :

1. What happens if I reset the program and enter two fairly large numbers such as e.g. 60 and 61 ? You should see a value of 121 in the output.
2. What if the first number you try to enter is 999 and the second number you try to enter is also 999 ? You should see that the output is -1, and that the accumulator displays a value of -001. Is this some kind of error or is it because of the way numbers are added inside the little man computer ?

3. What happens if you reset the program yet again and now try and enter a four digit number when prompted ? You should see a dialog with an error message "Bad input - number out of range". You can alter the number to something in the valid range (0 to 999) and continue.

Fig 2.5 Out of Range Input Error Dialog

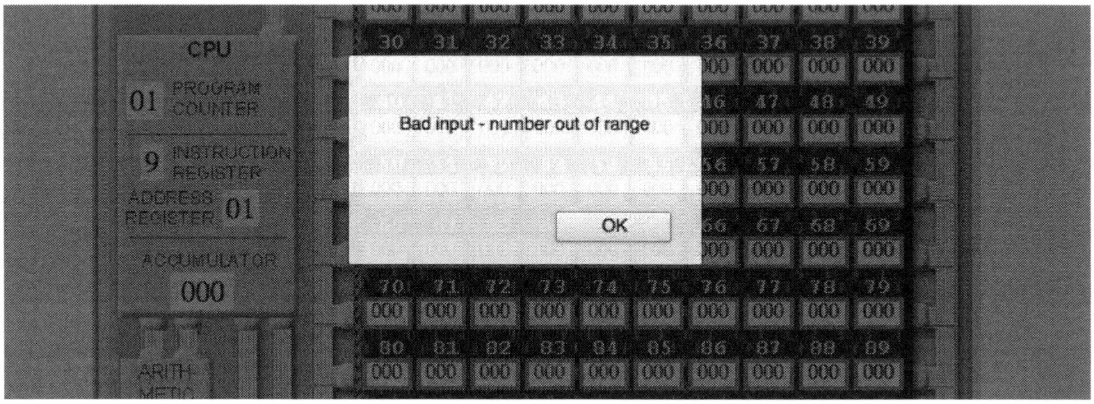

4. Experiment a little further and try adding two numbers that add up to a value that is bigger than 1000. What does the accumulator display ? Why do you get different values for different inputs that add up to different numbers that exceed 1000 ?

e.g.

- 555 + 555 gives -889
- 511 + 511 gives -977

Experiment with more numbers and see if you can discern some kind of pattern.

When writing computer programs it is essential to test them out thoroughly. For example if you have a program that adds two numbers you cannot assume that a user of that program will enter two numbers whose sum is less than 1000. What happens if you try and enter negative numbers ?

In this Little Man Computer simulation it seems that the Little Man Computer can handle negative numbers, e.g. (-55) + (-44) gives -99 and that the mailboxes can also store negative numbers. Not all Little Man Computer simulations show this behaviour, and it is apparent that the Higginson Little Man Computer has extended the capabilities of the original Mark 1 Little Man Computer.

The moral, of course is, "Make sure you know the capabilities and limitations of the computer you are working with".

2.3.2 Basic Addition and Subtraction.

The program we have just studied that does addition can be easily modified to do subtraction. All that we need do is to replace the ADD instruction with a SUB instruction. The Little Man Computer can run programs that use addition and subtraction together in the same program. The following example, 'add/subtr' , that comes with the Higginson Little Man Computer simulator demonstrates this quite nicely.

Table 2.2 'add/subtr' Program Showing Mailbox contents with descriptions

Mailbox Address	Instruction	Instruction in Assembler	Description
00	901	INP	Input first number
01	309	STA 09	Store it at address 9
02	901	INP	Input second number
03	109	ADD 09	Add number stored at address 09 (the first number entered) to it
04	902	OUT	Output the result
05	901	INP	Input third number - this is the number now held in the accumulator
06	209	SUB 09	Subtract number stored at address 09 (the first number entered)
07	902	OUT	Output the result
08	000	HLT	HALT
09	000	DAT	DATA held here.

This simple little program takes three numbers as input. It display the sum of the first two numbers, and then it displays the result of subtracting the first number from the second number.

To explore this program and to test it out requires trying various kinds of input including positive numbers as well as negative numbers.

2.3.3 Basics of branching operations.

Branching instructions are the basis for implementing if - then - else logic in computer programs. A branch instruction is one that can result in the value of the program counter changing arbitrarily. They are very powerful, but also potentially very dangerous. Undisciplined use of branching instructions can result in code that is difficult to understand and which may also contain subtle bugs (errors). This section will simply illustrate some basic uses of branching operations. In the next chapter we will explore structured programming using pseudocode and flowchart techniques and discover more complex usage patterns involving branching instructions that become possible when branching instructions are combined with counters.

The 'max' example that comes with the Higginson Little Man Computer illustrates the basic approach to working with branching instructions. In this example a user inputs two numbers, and the program outputs the larger of those two numbers.

The program is shown in table 2.3 .

This program is still difficult to read. However, if we use labels to represent addresses (locations) in memory, (and the Higginson Little Man Computer knows how to work with labels) then the Assembler is much easier to follow, as labels, if given meaningful names, are much easier to understand than raw numeric addresses.

Here is the program written in assembler which includes the use of labels.

```
          INP
          STA FIRST
          INP
          STA SECOND
          SUB FIRST
          BRP HIGHER
          LDA FIRST
          BRA DONE
HIGHER    LDA SECOND
DONE      OUT
          HLT
FIRST     DAT
SECOND    DAT  // Reads two input numbers and outputs the higher one.
```

Table 2.3 'max' Program Showing Mailbox contents with descriptions

Mailbox Address	Instruction	Instruction in Assembler	Description
00	901	INP	Input first number
01	311	STA 09	Store it at address 9
02	901	INP	Input second number
03	312	STA 12	Store the second number entered into address 12 (Remember that his value will still be in the accumulator).
04	211	SUB 11	Subtract the first number from the second number
05	808	BRP 08	If the result of subtracting the first number entered from the second number entered is positive go to address 8
06	511	LDA 11	Load the value at address 11 (the first number entered) into the accumulator (calculator).
07	609	BRA 9	Go to address 9
08	512	LDA 512	Load the value at address 12 (the second number entered) into the accumulator (calculator).
09	902	OUT	Output the greater number
10	000	HLT	Halt program
11		DAT	DATA held here.
12		DAT	DATA held here.

If we examine the assembler we can see that it uses both a conditional branching instruction (BRP) and an unconditional branching instruction (BRA). If the second number is smaller than or equal to the first number then the result of subtracting the first number from the second number will not be positive, so we must output the first number. In order to do this we must first load it into the accumulator before we can output it by jumping (unconditionally) to the instruction that does the outputting and which is located at the address associated with the symbol done. Otherwise we must output the first number.

In order to do this we have to skip past the code that loads the first number into the accumulator and jumps to the output instruction. The instruction for loading the second number into the accumulator is associated with the label HIGHER so this is where we must jump to. The two numbers are stored at addresses labeled, suitably enough, FIRST and SECOND.

In pseudocode we could have written the program as follows

```
Input the first number and save it
Input the second number and save it
If (second number - first number) is greater than 0 then
     Output the second number
Else
     Output the first number
Endif
```

Instead of using pseudocode to describe the program we could have used flowcharts, and this is the subject matter of the next chapter.

Chapter 2 Exercises and Projects

1. Do some research on the web and see if you can obtain other implementations of the Little Man Computer. In what respects do they differ from the Higginson Little Man Computer. An interesting implementation is one implemented in a dialect of basic called RTB that runs on the RaspberryPi and which can be found at the following URL https://projects.drogon.net/lmc/ . There are other implementations out there.

2. Write and test a program that adds up three numbers. In your solution you should provide

   - A pseudocode description of the code.
   - The assembly language program.
   - The machine code.
   - An account of how you tested your program. This should include situations where the user inputs negative as well as positive values, and situations where e.g. the sum of the first two numbers which are both positive yields an output which is negative.

3. Write and test a program which is given three positive numbers and outputs the highest of those three numbers. As with question 2 provide

   - A pseudocode description of the code.
   - The assembly language program.
   - The machine code.
   - An account of how you tested your program. This should include situations where the position of the highest number is at the beginning, at the middle and at the end, and also a situation where two of the numbers are the same.

CHAPTER 3
Designing Little Man Computer Programs Using Flowcharts and Pseudocode.

All computer programs contain the following implementation patterns

- SEQUENCE - Executing statements one after another
- CHOICE - Evaluating some condition and using the result to decide what piece of code to run next.
- REPETITION - Repeating a group of statements for a definite or, sometimes, indefinite number of times. When a group of statements is repeated an indefinite number of time this is referred to as an "infinite loop".

In complex code these patterns can be nested inside one another. For example a choice may lead to code in which there is a further choice and so on, or a repetition loop may have another repetition loop nested inside it. When code starts to get complex it is often useful to describe the structure of that code in a graphical manner e.g. by making use of flowcharts. A flowchart is, literally, a graphical description of a computer program. The use of flowcharts was one of the earliest techniques used to help in the design and understanding of complex computer programs. Before sophisticated graphical plotters and graphical user interfaces became available flowcharts were drawn by hand, sometimes with the use of stencils to make the various flowchart symbols look neat.

For relatively small programs such as those designed for the Little Man Computer the corresponding flowcharts can be drawn by hand. However, in order to produce good looking reports and presentations it is useful to make use of a suitable flowchart diagramming tool. Microsoft's Visio is an example of a widely used commercial diagramming tool. In this book we will, however, be using Dia, an open source diagramming tool that can be run on Microsoft Windows, or Linux or MACOSX computers.

3.1 Introduction to Flowcharts

A flowchart is a way of describing a process or procedure graphically. Flowcharts are useful for describing the behaviour of computer programs, administrative procedures, processes for organising and collecting data, and, also business processes. Here, of course, we will be focusing on the use of flowcharts for describing computer programs.

The word 'graphically' has two aspects to it

1. Producing a drawing (a graphical object)
2. A graph in the computing sense as a collection of shapes (nodes) joined together by lines (arcs). The shapes and lines can have text associated with them that describe what they mean.

The basic flowchart symbols used for describing computer programs (algorithms) are those shown in the table below.

Table 3.1 Basic Flowchart Symbols for Describing Computer Programs.

Symbol	Name	Description
	Flow line	Used to show the flow of logic between connected symbols.
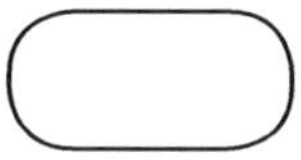	Terminal(Stop/Start)	Used to denote (show) the start or end of a flowchart.
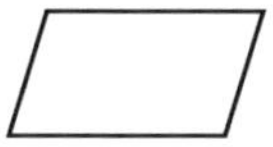	Input/Output	Used to denote an input or an output operation.
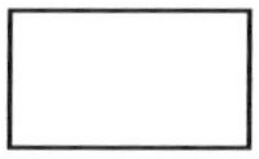	Processing	Used to denote and describe data manipulation or arithmetic operations that take place in this part of the algorithm.
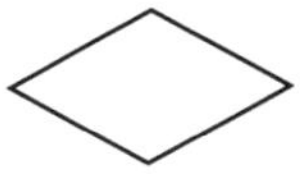	Decision	Used to denote an operation in which there are two alternatives, true and false. The alternative taken depends on whether the logical expression in the Decision diamond evaluates to true or false.
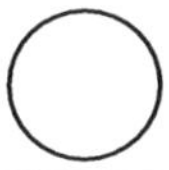	On-page Connector	Used to connect together several flowlines.
	Off-page Connector	Used to connect from this flowchart to another flowchart portion on different page. Useful when the flowchart is complex and you wish to provide a high level flowchart and delegate (move) the details to flowchart portions drawn on separate pages.
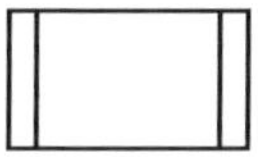	Predefined Process/ Function	Used denote a group of statements that perform a single piece of processing that make up a particular processing task.

A well designed and well drawn flowchart should be easy to follow. A really good test of a flowchart is to give it to someone else and ask them to explain what is being described in the flowchart.

If you search the internet you will find many examples of flowcharts describing various procedures or algorithms. Depending on the tool used to draw the diagrams details as to colouring, fonts, how sharp or rounded corners are may vary from tool to tool. This is generally a matter of "taste". Some users want to be able to produce more “artistic and colourful” flowcharts e.g. for presentation purposes.

Here is an example flowchart describing an algorithm ,for adding the first 50 integers, drawn using Edrawsoft’s diagramming tool [6]

Fig 3.1 A Flowchart Diagram describing an algorithm to add the first 50 numbers

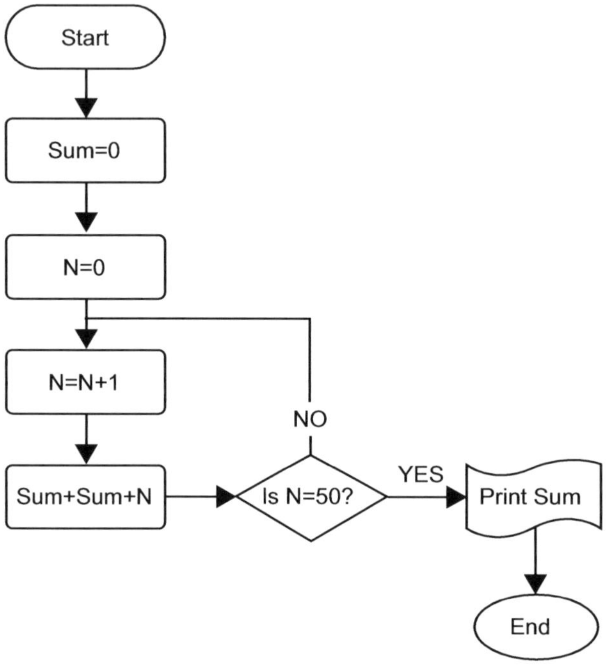

3.2 Installing Dia and Drawing Flowcharts with Dia.

Installation of Dia is not particularly difficult. The download page at http://dia-installer.de/download/index.html has tabs for Windows, Linux and MACOSX. You simply select the operating system on which Dia is to run, make a note of any installation requirements and download the Dia installer for your chosen operating system. Once downloaded run the installer and check that Dia works. On the newer versions of MACOSX in order for Dia to run it will be necessary to install XQuartz, an implementation of X11 Windows for MACOSX that Dia requires.

Dia is a typical integrated development environment and has many subwindows, toolbars, menus as well as an editing area. The various shapes and lines are generated by dragging a shape from the shapes collection, or a line from the line objects (straight lines, zig-zag line with right angles, curved lines ...) and then adjusting its size.

Fig 3.2 Dia Flowchart Drawing

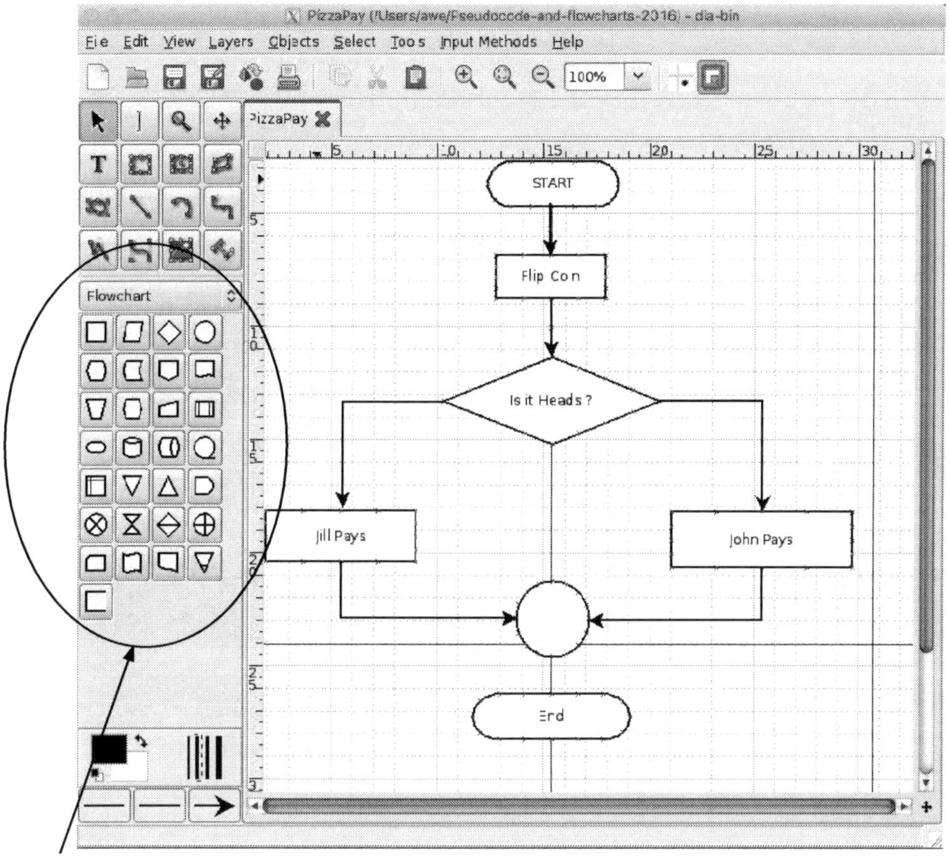

Flowchart Shapes

Right clicking on a line or shape brings up a properties dialog box which allows background colour, border and other properties to be set. You will notice / discover that in addition to colour you can specify whether the corners are rounded or not, text font and text size and lots of other properties. Usually it pays to keep things simple.

Fig 3.3 Editing the Properties of a Box Object Dialog

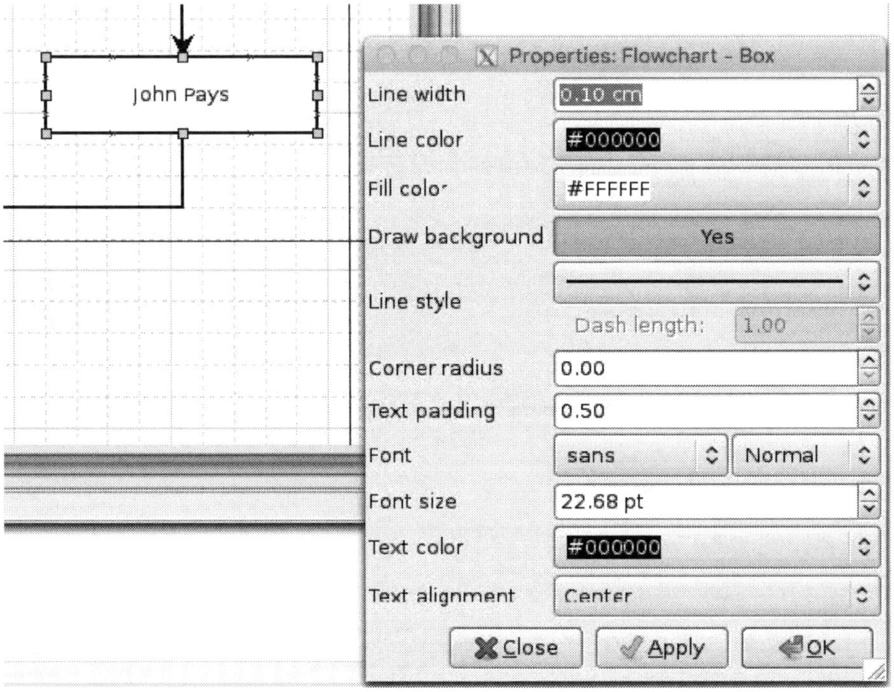

3.2.1 Rules for Flowcharts

- The symbols of the flowchart are connected by flow lines (these have a direction - as indicated by the arrow at the end of the line i.e. it is not a plain line.)
- Flowlines enter at the top of the symbol and exit out at the bottom, except for
  - The Decision symbol, which can have flow lines exiting from the bottom or the sides.
  - The on page connector, which can have flow lines entering at the sides.
- Flowcharts should usually be drawn so that the flow is from top to bottom
- The beginning and the end of the flowchart is indicated using the Terminal symbol.

3.3. Pseudocode

In order for flowcharts to be useful there has to be some way of going from a flowchart description to writing some Little Man Computer assembler. Sequence , where a sequence of basic operations is concerned is easy. Branching and making decisions is harder, and looping is harder still. Nevertheless in order to become proficient programmers we must master the techniques of converting choices sketched out in our flowchart into assembler code. Furthermore we must also master how to describe loops in a flowchart, and then, how to convert such looping flowchart constructs into assembler code.

It turns out that, in order to go from flowchart to assembler we need to understand how to set up and use labels and variables when writing assembler code. This is not nearly as frightening as it might seem, but it is important to differentiate between a code label and a variable.

A code label is simply a label for some location in memory that holds an instruction.

A variable is simply a label for some location in memory that holds data.

It is up to us to know which locations hold instructions and which hold data so that we do not accidentally ovewrite a piece of data with an instruction, or, overwrite an instruction with a piece of data.

3.3.1 Pseudocode - the Language

Pseudocode is sometimes referred to as “structured English” (at least in English speaking countries). It is simply a means of describing an algorithm semi-informally in words. There has been much discussion on the relative merits of flowcharts vs. pseudocode, however, both have “their uses”. To some extent it may depend on personal taste. Some programmers seem to find it easier to describe certain algorithms in pseudocode rather than flowcharts, and there are other programmers who are almost exclusively committed to flowcharts. As is often the case with such things you will need to discover what works best for you, both individually, and in a team context.

For pseudocode to be used effectively the key word is the word “structured” in “structured English”. In addition a number of computer programming borrowed words need to be used, as pseudocode is a kind of hybrid language that lies between English and a computer programming language.

The origins of pseudocode are to be found in the work of computer scientists Corrado Böhm and Giuseppe Jacopini who, in 1966, were some of the early pioneers who demonstrated that all programs could be written using three control structures: Sequence, Selection, and Repetition [7].

Noting that a programming language statement is the smallest part of a computer program that can be used , i.e. that a program is a collection of statements, it is possible to provide a more formal description of what makes a programming language.

Böhm and Jacopini's definitions of programming language structures can be summarised as follows :

- A sequence structure is a construct where one statement is executed after another
- A selection structure is a construct in which statements can be executed or skipped depending on whether some condition evaluates to TRUE or FALSE
    - The C programming language, from which many other languages such as C++, Java and C# are based has three selection structures :
    1. IF
    2. IF - ELSE
    3. SWITCH
    - The SWITCH statement can be used in pseudocode, but it is not necessary as the logic of a SWITCH statement can be expressed using IF - ELSE. So, we will not be exploring the SWITCH statement here.
- A repetition structure is a construct in which statements can be executed repeatedly until a condition evaluates to TRUE or FALSE
    - The C programming language provides three repetition structures
    1. WHILE
    2. DO – WHILE
    3. FOR
- The FOR loop can be used in pseudocode, but it is not necessary as the logic of a FOR loop can be captured by a combination of regular statements and the use of WHILE or DO - WHILE loops.

In the pseudocode that will be presented in this book we will make use of

- IF
- IF - ELSE
- WHILE
- DO - WHILE

We can describe pseudocode (which is also know as Program Design Language in some circles) as follows :

Pseudocode

- Is a description of a program made up of natural language-like statements that precisely and correcly describe the steps of an algorithm or program
- The statements describe actions - things that will be performed / executed
- The pseudocode focuses on the logic of the algorithm or program and
    - Avoids the language-specific elements and syntax of any particular programming language, i.e.
- Pseudocode is portable and a pseudocode description can be translated into almost any computer programming language, including assembly language.

- The level of detail in the pseudocode is such that it should, in theory, be possible to generate the required code in a chosen programming language almost automatically from the pseudocode statements provided.
- The steps/statements can be numbered.
  - Where statements are contained in selection / repetition structures indentation, or the use of subordinate numbers can be used to show that these statements belong to a group of statements associated with a particular selection or repetition structure.

Some programmers, when writing pseudocode will add an ending 'keyword' on a separate line to make it quite clear where a particular selection or repetition structure ends. You may come across terms such as ENDIF or ENDWHILE used for just such a purpose. Whilst some programming languages have keywords such as ENDIF or ENDWHILE, other languages e.g. members of the C family of programming languages do not. Use of ENDIFs and ENDWHILEs can add considerably to the length of a large piece of pseudocode. For normal sized programs the use of ENDIFs and ENDWHILEs can be very helpful, especially in spotting errors where there are several levels of nesting.

This is all very formal, and not nearly as bad as it seems, as the sections and examples that follow will, hopefully, demonstrate. Appendix 1. describes the PDL language, and Appendix 2 describes the pseudocode language dialect that will be used in this book.

3.4 How to go from flowcharts and pseudocode to Little Man Computer Assembler

The key to success is to understand and master the underlying patterns. In programming parlance a pattern is a piece of code that is associated with providing a solution to a certain kind of problem. To become proficient in assembly language programming the key ability is to be able to see the way code needs to be structured and written to implement selection (IF - ELSE) and repetition (WHILE and DO - WHILE). This is what we will focus on here. Once having mastered how to convert IF - ELSE , WHILE and DO - WHILE statements into Little Man Computer assembler code the path is clear to implementing more complex code for e.g. creating and manipulating collections of data such as arrays, for example. An array is simply a collection of values held in successive addresses in memory. The kinds of things that can be done with an array of values include

- Finding the largest / smallest element in the array.
- Adding up the values of all the numbers in an array of numbers.
- Sorting the numbers in an array in either ascending or descending order.

In order to be able to write assembler programs that solve these kinds of problem it is first necessary to know now to write assembler to produce IF - ELSE , WHILE, and DO - WHILE behaviour.

3.4.1 Challenge 1. How to implement an IF - ELSE statement using Little Man Computer assembler

To make this challenge concrete we will explore the implementation of a Little Man Computer program that reads in two numbers and stores them in memory. It then compares these two numbers and outputs a 1 if the first number is greater than or equal to the second number, and outputs a 0 if the first number is less than or equal to the second number.

There are various ways of implementing such a program that may vary in either memory usage or efficiency. When getting started on a problem an important attitude / approach is GIWF (Get It Working First). Once you have a , hopefully reasonable, working solution, you can consider trying to optimise it for speed or memory usage or both. However another thing worth remembering is that optimising a program aggressively can make it difficult to understand and maintain. So don't worry about coming up with the fastest or most memory efficient solution first. With experience you will pick up problem solving and code structuring techniques that are not explicitly documented anywhere. Programming is one of those subjects that combines elements of both science and art.

In answer to the question as to whether you should start off with pseudocode first, or with flowcharts first my answer is "go with what, to you, seems to fit best for the problem at hand" , unless, of course you are told to specifically use one approach or the other. Even then you can "secretly" (unless you are being closely observed) use your preferred option and then use that, if it turns out to be the case that you are required to do so, to turn out the "required" option.

In our pseudocode comments will start with a pair of forward slashes // and continue to the end of the line. This is a common convention for programming languages such as C, C++, C# and Java.

Pseudocode program for challenge 1.

```
define variable num1 // for holding first number
define variable num2 // for holding second number
Input number
Store input in num1
Input number
Store input in NUM2
IF num1 >=  num2 // >= is stands for greater than or equal to
      OUTPUT 1
ELSE
      OUTPUT 0
ENDIF
HALT
```

Fig 3.4 Flowchart for challenge 1

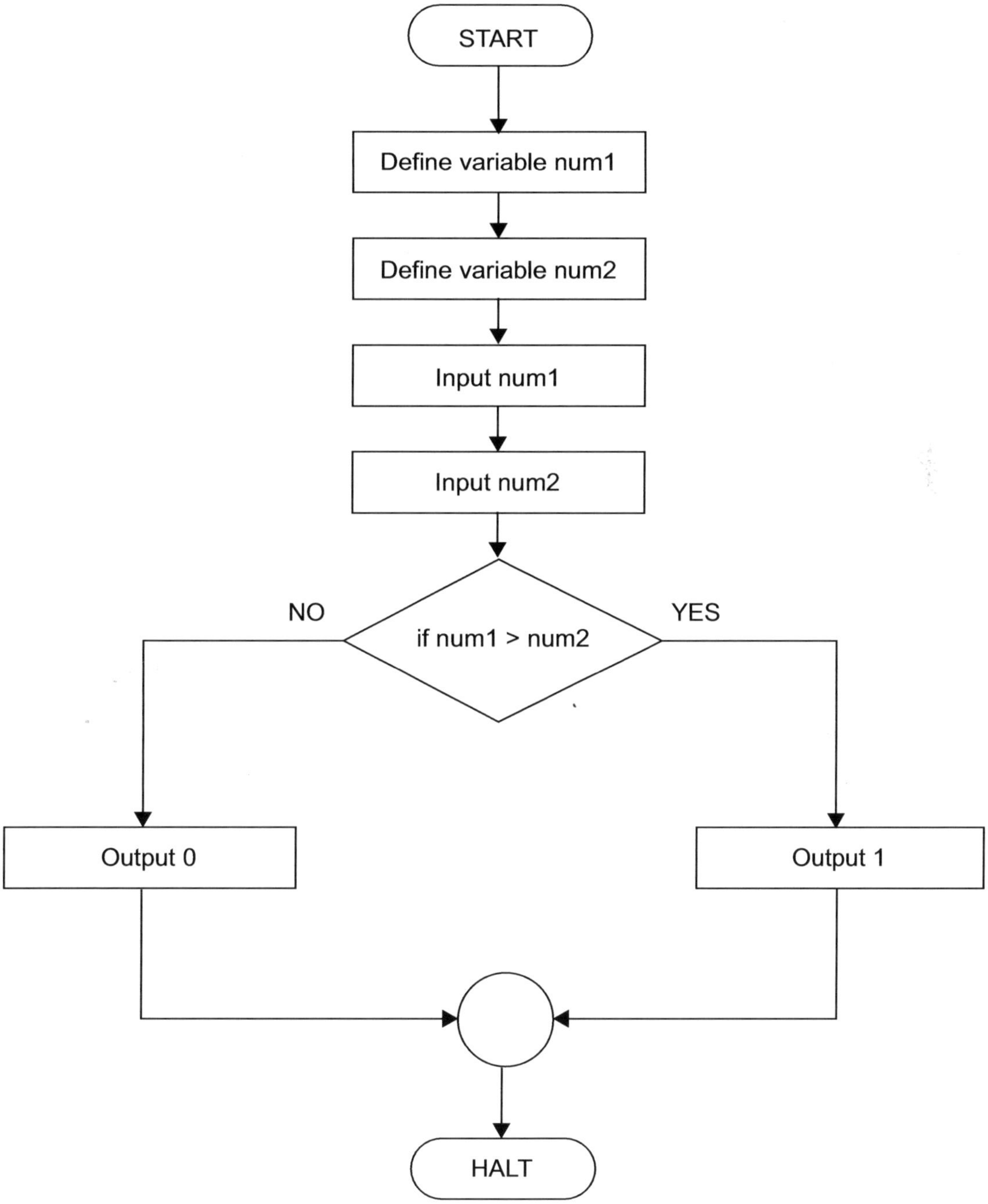

We now need to convert these programs into Little Man Computer assembler.

In order to do this we need to work out

1. How to define variables in Little Man Computer assembler.
2. How to write the assembler that will compute whether num1 is greater than num2 and then branch to produce an output of 1 if num1 is greater than num2 or branch to produce an output of 0 if this is not the case.
3. Halt the program.

Defining variables in Little Man Computer assembler can be accomplished by the use of labels and the DAT directive. Lets start by simply writing a little program that reads in two numbers and saves them to memory. The assembler with labels and data (DAT) directives is shown on the left and the resulting assembler with labels resolved is shown on the right. The memory address of each instruction is shown. Looking at the final assembler code you can see that num1 corresponds to memory location 05 and num2 corresponds to memory location 06.

Fig 3.5 Assembler for reading in and storing two numbers

```
            INP
            STA num1
            INP
            STA num2
            HLT
num1        DAT
num2        DAT
```

```
00 INP
01 STA 05
02 INP
03 STA 06
04 HLT
05 DAT 00
06 DAT 00
```

Running the program and entering e.g. 33 for the value of the first number and 22 for the value of the second number will result in the value 33 being written to mailbox 5 and the value 22 being written to mailbox 6. If the program was extended and further instructions were added before the data definitions for num1 and num2 the assembler will deduce the correct mailbox locations associated with the symbols num1 and num2, you do not have to "count the mailboxes".

The next sub-problem to tackle is how to realise the branching logic. The only branching operations are the conditional branching instructions that depend on the value in the accumulator, and the absolute branch instruction BA. The conditional branching instructions are BRP (Branch to the address given by the operand if the number in the accumulator is greater than zero) , and BRZ (Branch to the address given in the operand if the number in the accumulator is zero). There is no BRN (Branch on Negative) instruction.

To compare num1 and num2 we load num1 into the accumulator and then subtract num2 from it.

If the result is positive we output a 1, otherwise we output a 0. To do this we must solve the following problems

1. The Little Man Computer does not have any instructions that will load an absolute value into the accumulator. The value to be loaded into the accumulator has to be fetched from a mailbox. This means that we need a mailbox containing a 0 and another mailbox containing a 1. We can either enter the constant values for 'zero' and 'one' at the start of the program, or, we can make use of the fact that we can edit the contents of mailboxes directly before running the program. Editing the mailboxes directly is the approach that will be demonstrated here. We need to set up the mailboxes that will hold zero (0) and one (1) but only edit their contents after our assembled program has been loaded into memory. This is because the program that loads the code will zero out all the other unused mailboxes as a precaution.

2. The next problem to solve is that if we need to output a 0 we need to jump past the code that will output a 1. This requires the use of an absolute branch instruction to jump to the code immediated after the block that outputs a 1.

Lets take a look at the assembler code using labels and the assembly code it produces with all the label symbols resolved (mapped to their actual addresses).

Fig 3.6 Assembler for Challenge 1

```
        INP
        STA num1
        INP
        STA num2
        LDA num1
        SUB num2
        BRP out1
        LDA zero
        OUT
        BRA stop
out1    LDA one
        OUT
stop    HLT
zero    DAT
one     DAT
num1    DAT
num2    DAT
```

```
00 INP
01 STA 15
02 INP
03 STA 16
04 LDA 15
05 SUB 16
06 BRP 10
07 LDA 13
08 OUT
09 BRA 12
10 LDA 14
11 OUT
12 HLT
13 DAT 00
14 DAT 00
15 DAT 00
16 DAT 00
```

By looking at the two listings above you can work out that zero is at address 13 and one is at address 14. We want that contents of mailbox 13 to be 000 , which is the case immediately after the code has been assembled into RAM. The contents of mailbox 14 are also 000. So, we have to edit it directly by clicking inside it and typing in a 1.

The contents of the mailbox after we have performed this edit now will look as follows :

Fig 3.7 Little Man Computer with code for Challenge 1 with Data in Mailbox 14 set to 001.

The program can now be tested. The following screen capture shows the result output when the first number entered is 33 and the second number entered is 22. The value 33 is in mailbox 15 and the value 22 is in mailbox 16. The output is 1.

Fig 3.8 Challenge 1 Output for num1 33 and num2 22

In the following screen capture shows the result output when the first number entered is 22 and the second number entered is 33. The value 22 is in mailbox 15 and the value 33 is in mailbox 16. The output is 0.

Fig 3.9 Challenge 1 Output for num1 22 and num2 33

An alternative to editing the contents of the mailbox is to enter a constant data value. This is because in the Little Man Computer assembler DAT can be followed by a literal value e.g.

```
zero  DAT  0
one   DAT  1
```

3.4.2 Challenge 2. How to implement a WHILE loop in Little Man Computer assembler.

A while loop continues executing code in the body of the loop (the subordinate instructions / statements in the loop) till some condition fails to be true, or some instruction inside the loop triggers a branch out of the loop. A typical simple WHILE loop involves

- A counter variable
- A condition involving that counter variable that is used to decide whether to exit from the loop or not.
- Some code inside the loop that modifies the counter variable.

Again, as a concrete challenge, we will attempt to create a program that will add up the first 20 integers from 1 to 20 inclusive.

In pseudocode we might do this something as follows :

```
define a variable sumOfInts
define a variable counter
initialise sumOfInts to 0
initialise counter to 0
WHILE counter < 20
      counter = counter + 1
      sumOfInts = sumOfInts + counter
ENDWHILE
output sumOfInts
STOP
```

The corresponding flowchart might look something as follows :

Fig 3.10 Flowchart for Challenge 2

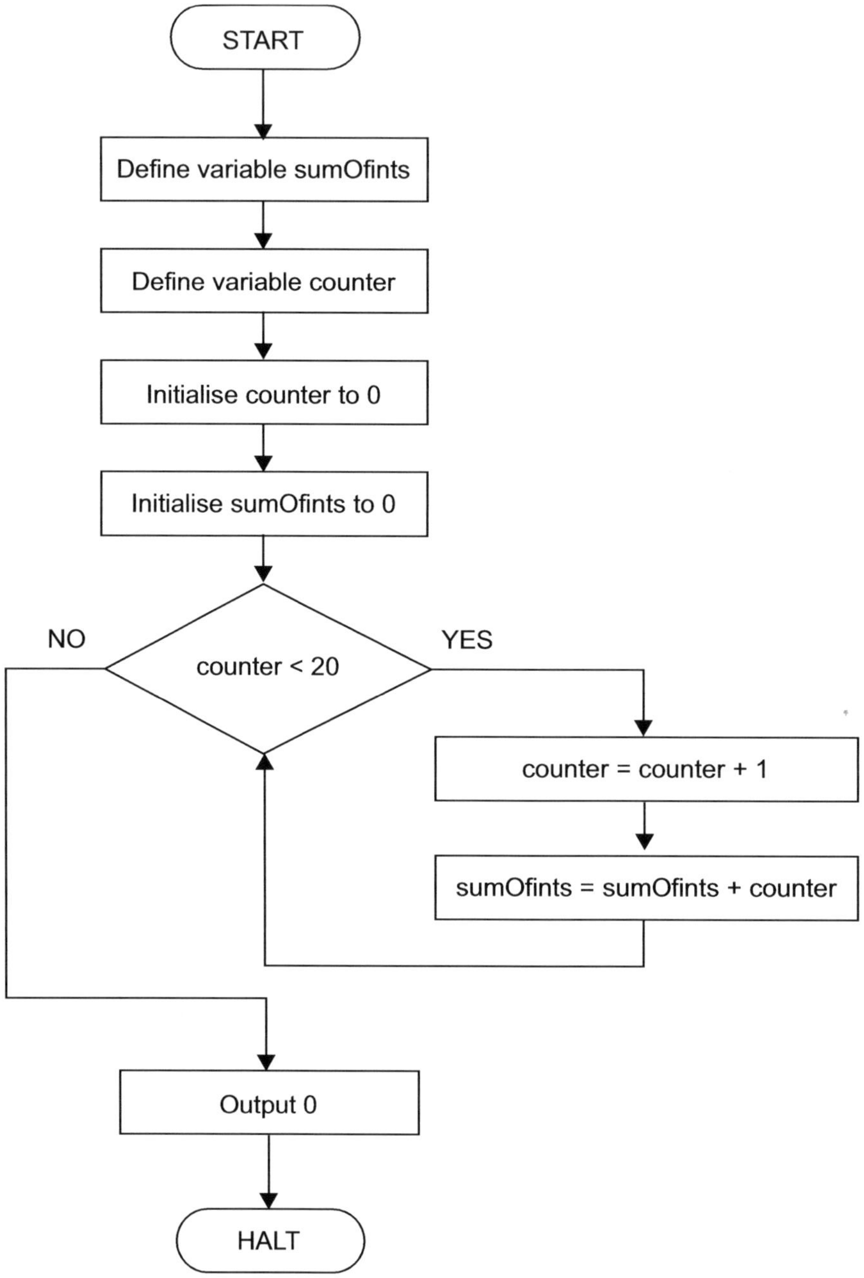

Fig 3.11 Assembler for Challenge 2

loop	LDA numToCount
	SUB counter
	BRZ endLoop
	LDA sumOfInts
	ADD counter
	STA sumOfInts
	LDA counter
	ADD one
	STA counter
	BRA loop
endLoop	LDA sumOfInts
	OUT
stop	HLT
zero	DAT 0
one	DAT 1
sumOfInts	DAT 0
counter	DAT 0
numToCount	DAT 20

```
00 LDA 17
01 SUB 16
02 BRZ 10
03 LDA 15
04 ADD 16
05 STA 15
06 LDA 16
07 ADD 14
08 STA 16
09 BRA 00
10 LDA 15
11 OUT
12 HLT
13 DAT 00
14 DAT 01
15 DAT 00
16 DAT 00
17 DAT 20
```

Examining the above assembler, the pseudocode and the flowchart you should be able to work out that

1. The test for loop termination involves the 3 instructions

```
LDA numToCount
SUB counter
BRZ endLoop
```

When the counter value reaches 20 the last number added to the sumOfInts was 20.
This is because we increment the counter before adding it to the sumOfInts.
Hence as the counter value increases in the sequence 0,1,2 19
The value being added to the sumOfInts each time round the loop increases in the sequence 1,2,3,....20 . If we had started with an initial counter value of 1 and added the counter value to the sum of ints before incrementing it then the counter value would increase in the sequence 1,2,3, ...20. However, now we would have to terminate the loop when the counter value reaches 21. These kinds of "out by one" errors crop up all the time, and this is one reason why code needs to be carefully tested, so as to catch and fix such errors.

The body of the loop is quite straightforward basically it involves incrementing the counter and then adding the counter value to the sumOfInts, and then, finally branching back to the start of the loop via a BRA loop instruction.

The next instruction after the BRA loop instruction is the first instruction outside the while loop, and this is where the BRZ endLoop instruction takes us.

The formula for the sum of N integers is N * (N + 1) / 2

For N equal to 20 the sum is 210.

If you run the example on the Higginson Little Man Computer the output will be as shown in the following screen capture.

Fig 3.12 Challenge 2 - Output for sum of the 1st 20 integers.

3.4.3 Challenge 3. How to implement a DO - WHILE loop in Little Man Computer assembler .

In a DO - WHILE loop the test for loop termination, as already mentioned, occurs at the end of the body of the loop. DO - WHILE loops are used where the code that forms the body of the loop must be executed at least once .

To illustrate the use of DO - WHILE loop we will implement a Little Man Computer program that will count from 1 up to some specified non zero positive number, outputting a number each time round the loop.

The pseudocode for this example might be something as follows ... we have added the keyword DO to the set of pseudocode keywords. It does not have an ENDDO but rather has a terminating WHILE <some condition> .

```
Define a variable i
Define a variable max
Initialise i to 0
Initialise max to 11
DO
      i = i + 1
      output i
WHILE i < max
HALT
```

The corresponding flowchart might be drawn as follows :

Fig 3.13 Flowchart for Challenge 3 - DO - WHILE loop example

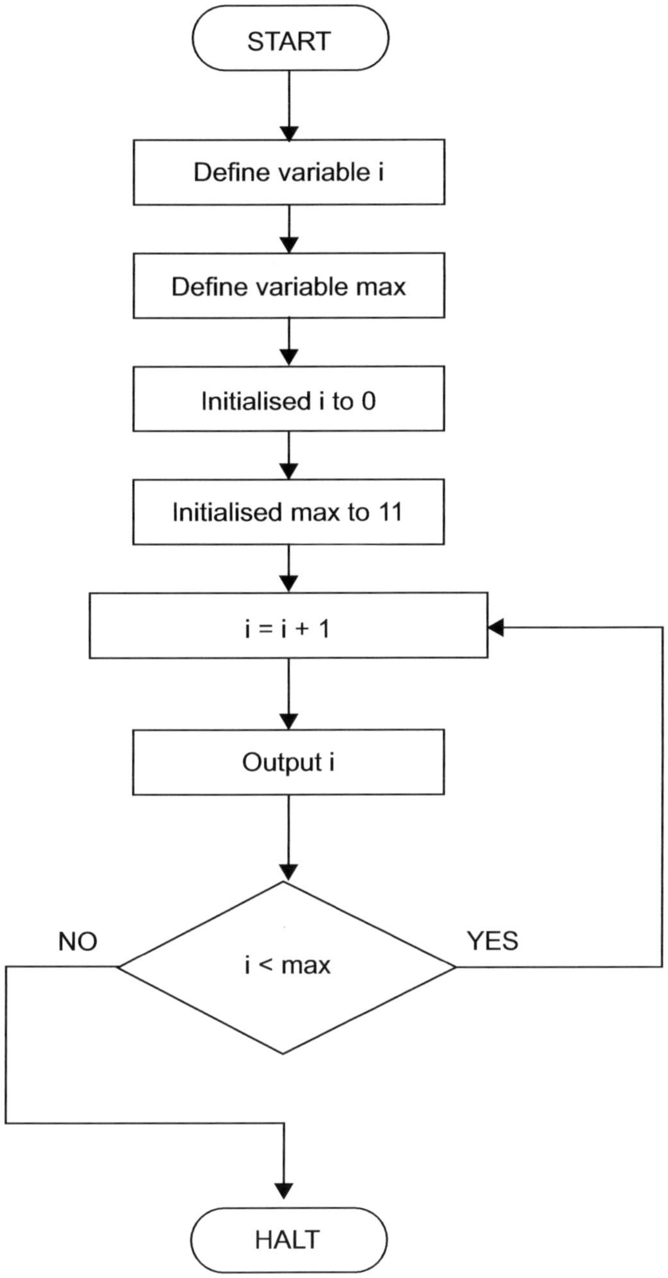

Now for the assembler. Here we have to be careful if we are going to use a BRP instruction, because in the Higginson Little Man Computer BRP means "Branch if zero or positive". This means that if we are to count up to 11 we must terminate the loop when i reaches the value 10 (maxSubOne in the assembler below) on entry into the body of the loop. When i has the value 10 on entering the body of the loop it will be incremented by 1 to give the value 11 and the value 11 will be output. The loop termination test which depends on whether the value of (maxSubOne - i) is less than 0 or not will now fail as (10 - 11) is -1. So here again an example of a potential "out by one" error for the unwary.

Fig 3.14 Challenge 3 DO - WHILE loop example - counting numbers - assembly listings

startLoop	LDA i
	ADD one
	STA i
	OUT
	LDA maxSubOne
	SUB i
	BRP startLoop
stop	HLT
one	DAT 1
zero	DAT 0
i	DAT 0
maxSubOne	DAT 10

00 LDA 10
01 ADD 08
02 STA 10
03 OUT
04 LDA 11
05 SUB 10
06 BRP 00
07 HLT
08 DAT 01
09 DAT 00
10 DAT 00
11 DAT 10

The screen capture below shows the output of the program. Note that the value in the accumulator is -1 , the result of subtracting 11 from 10.

Fig 3.15 Screen capture showing output and accumulator and register values for the numbers counting DO - WHILE loop example

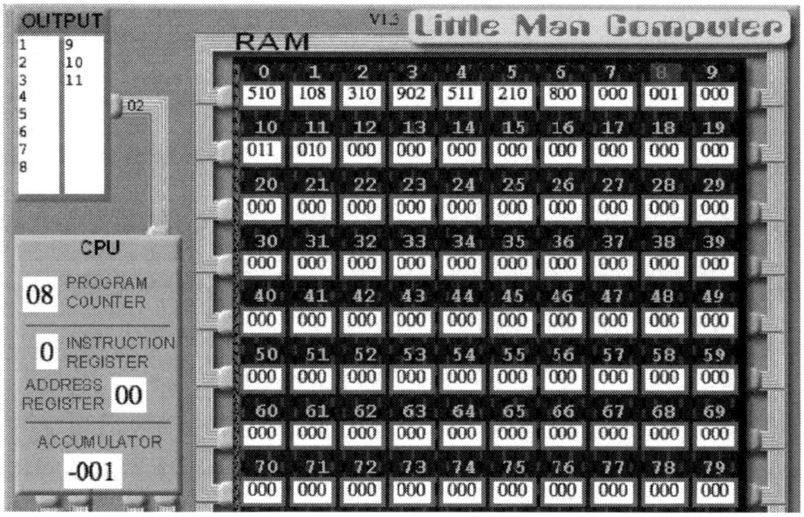

3.4.4 Challenge 4. How to implement nested IF - ELSE statements in Little Man Computer assembler.

For both the IF and ELSE part of an IF - ELSE statement it is perfectly possible for these parts to themselves contain an IF - ELSE statement. Also, an IF part does not, necessarily have to have an associated ELSE part. Where the number of ELSEs is less than the number of IFs it is very important to make sure that an ELSE is matched up with the correct IF.

The secret to success when writing nested IF - ELSE statements is to pay careful attention to the use of labels in the assembly code.

For this challenge the goal is to write a program that reads in two numbers and outputs

- 1 if the first number is greater than the second number.
- 0 if the two numbers are equal.
- -1 if the first number is smaller than the second number.

The pseudocode description of this program might be as follows.

```
Define a variable num1
Define a variable num2
Enter value for num1
Save entered value in num1
Enter value for num2
Save entered value in num2
IF num1 equal to num2
      OUTPUT 0
ELSE
      IF num1 > num2
            OUTPUT 1
      ELSE
            OUTPUT -1
      FI
FI
HALT
```

The flowchart might be as follows

Fig 3.16 Flowchart for challenge 4 - nested if - else

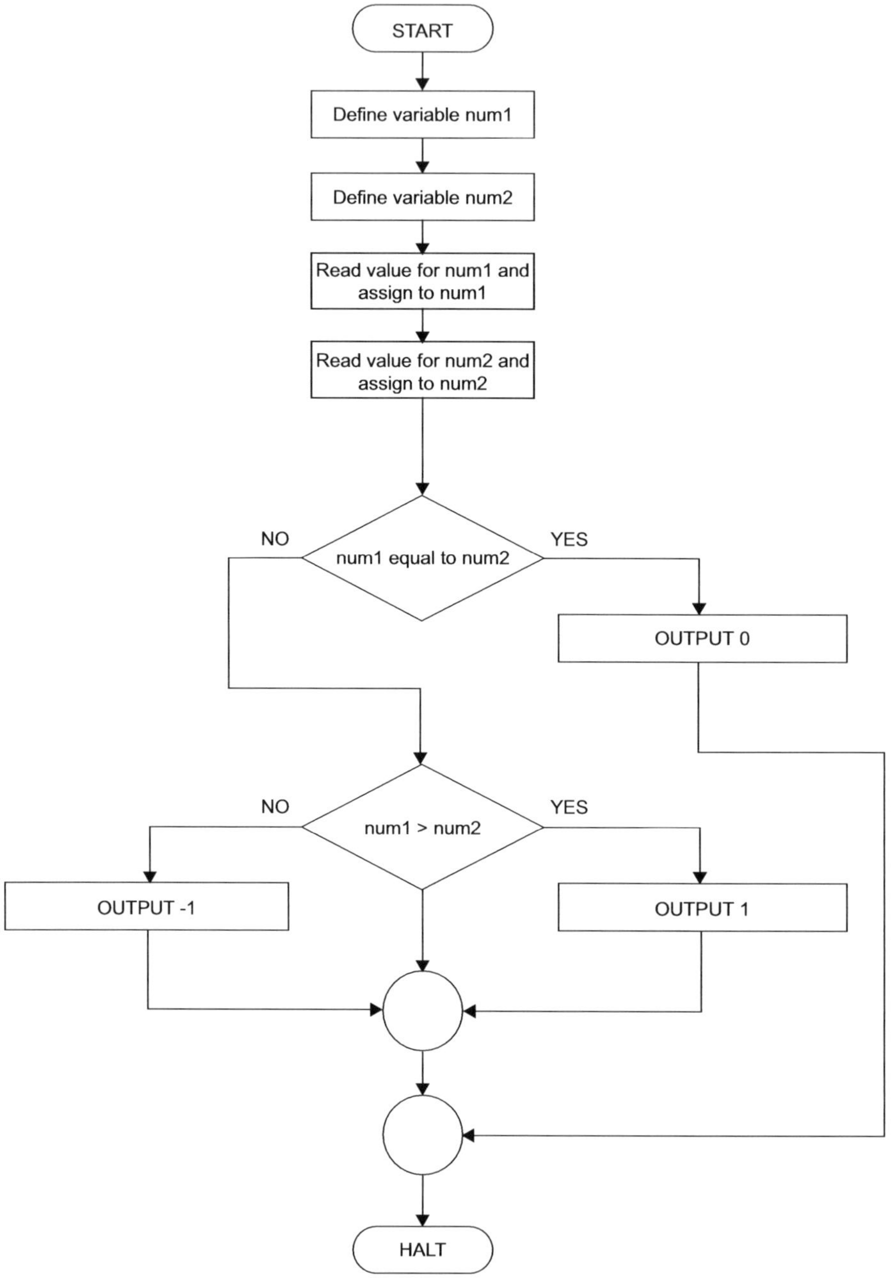

This program can be written in LMC assembler as follows:

Fig 3.17 Assembler for Challenge 4 - Nested IF - ELSE example

```
        INP
        STA num1
        INP
        STA num2
        LDA num1
        SUB num2
        BRZ equal
        BRP n1GTn2
        LDA zero
        SUB one
        OUT
        BRA stop
equal   LDA zero
        OUT
        BRA stop
n1GTn2  LDA one
        OUT
        BRA stop
        LDA zero
        SUB one
        OUT
stop    HLT
zero    DAT 0
one     DAT 1
num1    DAT
num2    DAT
```

```
00 INP
01 STA 24
02 INP
03 STA 25
04 LDA 24
05 SUB 25
06 BRZ 12
07 BRP 15
08 LDA 22
09 SUB 23
10 OUT
11 BRA 21
12 LDA 22
13 OUT
14 BRA 21
15 LDA 23
16 OUT
17 BRA 21
18 LDA 22
19 SUB 23
20 OUT
21 HLT
22 DAT 00
23 DAT 01
24 DAT 00
25 DAT 00
```

Because BRP branches when the contents in the accumulator are greater than or equal to zero it is necessary to first test for equality using BRZ and branch to the code that will output a zero. Immediately after this we test for greater than or equal to zero using BRP. If we reach this BRP we already know that the num1 and num2 are not equal, and so know , that if the BRP branch is taken that num1 is greater than num2, and , that if the BRP branch is not taken then num1 is less than num2.

Because the LMC can output negative numbers we can construct a -1 to output by putting 0 in the accumulator and then subtracting 1 from it.

The code then needs to be tested.

Although the assembler looks a bit complicated it really is quite logical. Early computers had fairly limited instruction sets and programmers of these early computers also had to, sometimes, resort to quite convoluted machine code to implement computer programs. As experience was gained so computer processors with richer instruction sets were developed. Eventually computer processors with large and complex instruction sets evolved. These were the CISC (Complex Instruction Set Computer) processor based computers. There were also forces at work leading to high performance processors with smaller instruction sets - the, so called, RISC (Reduced Instruction Set Computer) processor based computers. Most modern microcontrollers such as those from ARM or Microchip are RISC machines.

3.4.5 Challenge 5. How to implement nested WHILE loops in Little Man Computer assembler

Nested while loops occur very frequently when processing multi-dimensional data. An image can be thought of as a two dimensional array of pixel values and nested loops are frequently found in image processing applications.

The LMC does not have multiplication or division capabilities. Multiplication can be thought of as repeated addition. 3 times 3 for instance can be computed by adding 3 lots of 3 together. To implement a multiplication table on the LMC say from 1 times 4 through to 10 times 4 the outer loop would be used to step from 1 to 10 and the inner loop would be used to perform the multiplication by means of successive additions of the corresponding number in the table to achieve the result of performing a multiplication operation.

Pseudocode for multiplication table

```
Define variable size      // The size of the Times Table e.g. 10
                          // For a Times Table from 1 times X to 2 times X
Define variable mult      // The subject of the Times Table
                          // As in mult will have the value 4 in a 4 Times Table
Define variable counter   // Number of additions left
Define variable total     // Holds result of successive additions
Define variable curval    // The number being multiplied by mult
                          // e.g. for 2 x mult  VALUE is 2
Input value for  size
Save value in variable size
Input value for mult
Save value in variable mult
curval = 0
WHILE curval  <=  size
      curval = curval + 1
      counter = mult
      total = 0
      WHILE counter > 0
            total = total + curval
            counter = counter - 1 // Decrement  counter
      ENDWHILE
      OUTPUT total
ENDWHILE
HALT
```

Fig 3.18 Flowchart for multiplication table program - which illustrates nested WHILE loops.

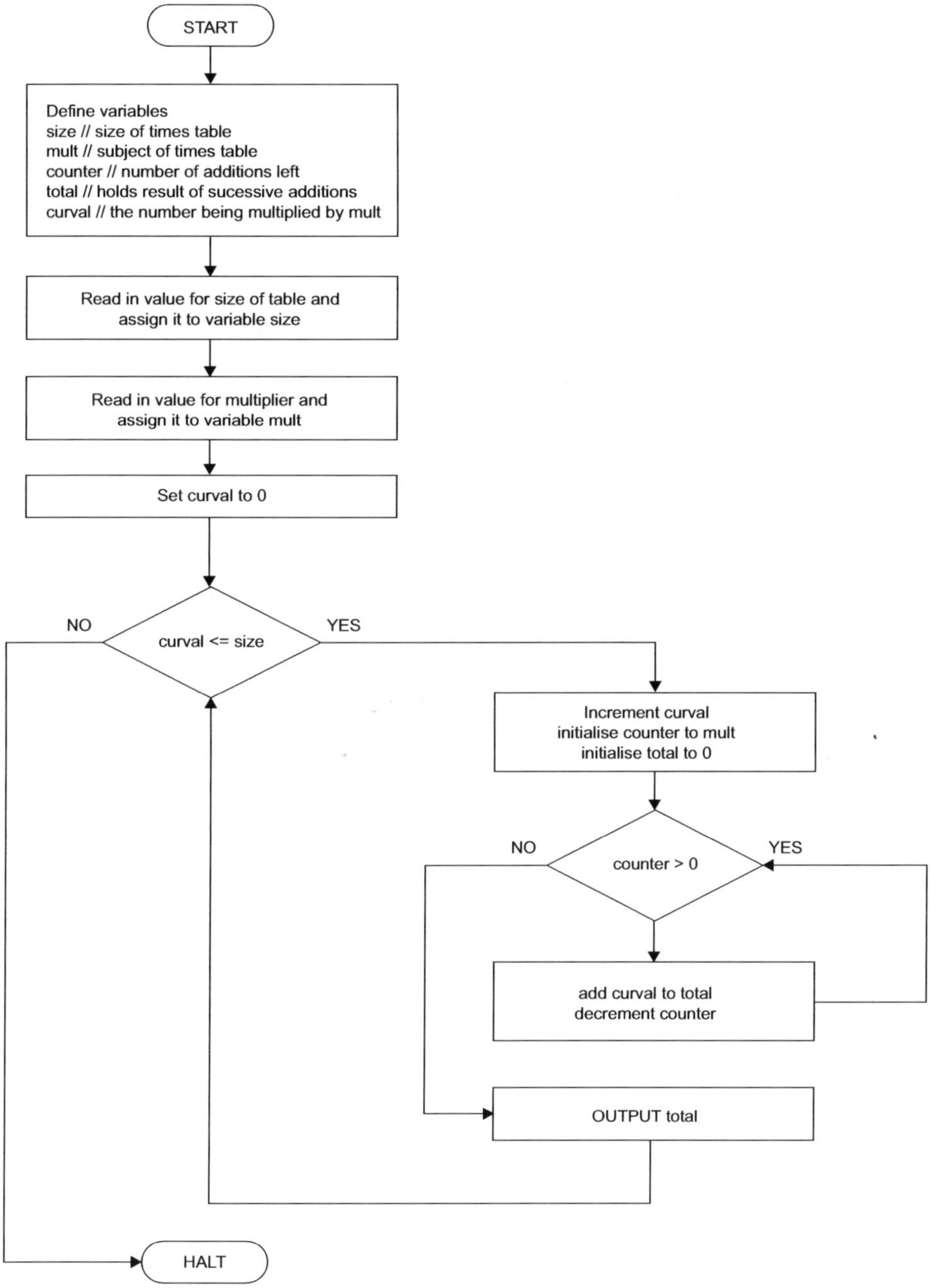

The assembler code should be studied in conjunction with the pseudocode and the flowchart. It is not too tricky but requires care. After a while spent programming you should start to identify commonly re-occurring themes and patterns. The ability to recognise and think with these patterns is referred to as "chunking" by some cognitive psychologists. It is a very useful mechanism for preventing brain overload, as you only drill down into the detail when you need to. Some structured programming practitioners refer to the strategy of sketching out a potential design at a high level as the "postponing of detail".

A screenshot of the output and the state of the LMC after outputting a the first 12 values of the 7 times multiplication table is shown below.

Fig 3.19 LMC Computer after outputting the first 12 values of the 7 times multiplication table

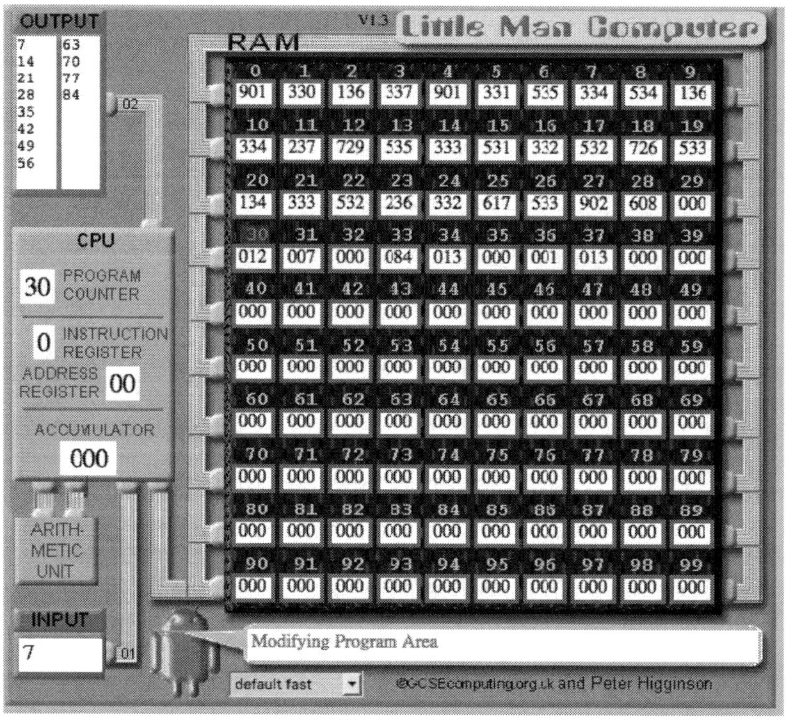

Assembler for the multiplication table program

```
           INP
           STA size
           ADD one
           STA endTable
           INP
           STA mult
           LDA zero
           STA curval
doTable    LDA curval
           ADD one
           STA curval
           SUB endTable
           BRZ done
           LDA zero
           STA total
           LDA mult
           STA counter
mulLoop    LDA counter
           BRZ outputVal
           LDA total
           ADD curval
           STA total
           LDA counter
           SUB one
           STA counter
           BRA mulLoop
outputVal  LDA total
           OUT
           BRA doTable
done       HLT
size       DAT 0
mult       DAT 0
counter    DAT 0
total      DAT 0
curval     DAT 0
zero       DAT 0
one        DAT 1
endTable   DAT 0
```

```
00 INP
01 STA 30
02 ADD 36
03 STA 37
04 INP
05 STA 31
06 LDA 35
07 STA 34
08 LDA 34
09 ADD 36
10 STA 34
11 SUB 37
12 BRZ 29
13 LDA 35
14 STA 33
15 LDA 31
16 STA 32
17 LDA 32
18 BRZ 26
19 LDA 33
20 ADD 34
21 STA 33
22 LDA 32
23 SUB 36
24 STA 32
25 BRA 17
26 LDA 33
27 OUT
28 BRA 08
29 HLT
30 DAT 00
31 DAT 00
32 DAT 00
33 DAT 00
34 DAT 00
35 DAT 00
36 DAT 01
37 DAT 00
```

CHAPTER 3
Excercises and Projects

1. Draw a flowchart that describes the following Posting a letter scenario.
    1. Write the letter.
    2. Put the letter in an envelope.
    3. Write the address of the recipient on the front of the envelope.
    4. Seal the envelope.
    5. Stick on a stamp in the top right corner.
    6. Put the envelope in the post box.

This is a description that leaves out many fine details such as e.g. finding an envelope or finding a stamp, or finding the post box. That is the point of working with flowcharts - you need to decide on the necessary level of detail.

2. Draw a flowchart that describes the following phoning a friend scenario.
    1. Select a friend to call from the friends list.
    2. Press the green call button.
    3. Wait for an answer.
    4. If no one answers after 20 seconds repeat steps 1 to 3 .
    5. Talk to your friend.

This is a description that. too, leaves out many fine details such as e.g. the details of interacting with you mobile phone's user interface, what to do if prompted to leave a voice message etc. ...

When working on problems an important principle to bear in mind is the KISS (Keep It Simple Stupid) principle. Basically it means devise the simplest solution that solves the problem at hand. This is particularly important when answering exam questions, or suggesting projects to work on.

3. Draw a flow chart that describes the details of the steps the Little Man follows in order to execute a branch (BRA) instruction. This flow chart should describe the details of where the little man walks to, what he does there etc.

4. Implement a program that will output the numbers between 1 and 100 that are divisible by 3.

Provide a flowchart and pseudocode as well as an actual implementation. There are several ways of doing this and some of them do not require an ability to be able to perform a divide by 3 operation.

5. Devise a Little Man Computer program that can read in an indefinite number of positive (i.e. greater than 0) numbers and output the largest number that has been input after the user has signaled that no more numbers will be entered. A user supplied value of 0 is used to indicate the end of the input of numbers.

6. The triangular numbers are the numbers whose value is the sum of the integers from 1 to N for some number N.

The sum of the integers from 1 to N is N * (N - 1) /2

If TN is the triangular number corresponding to N then the first few triangular numbers are
N = 1 TN = 1
N = 2 TN = 3
N = 3 TN = 6
N = 4 TN = 10
N = 5 TN = 15

In your program the user inputs a number.

The program outputs a 1 if the number is a triangular number, and also outputs the N that corresponds to that triangular number.

If the number is not a triangular number the output is 0.

Checking whether a number is a triangular number is more difficult than simply generating a triangular number. To solve this exercise careful thinking and well designed pseudocode / flowcharts will be essential.

CHAPTER 4

More Advanced LMC - Stretching the Little Man Computer a bit further.

A common requirement when developing computer programs is to create more complex collections of data out of basic data elements. In the case of the Little Man Computer the basic data type is a three digit decimal number. The other basic data type is the instruction. A mailbox does not care whether it contains a piece of numeric data or an instruction.

What we would like to do is to be able to create and manipulate collections of numbers, and, possibly collections of instructions. However, there is one problem and that is that so far we have not worked out how to compute addresses dynamically, and we need to be able to do this in order to extract from or insert into a piece of data in an array. Ideally we would like to be able to compute an LDA or an STA instruction by tagging on arbitrary address digits onto the instruction digit. We then need to put this instruction somewhere and to "point" the program counter to it so as to execute it. These are the puzzles we are going to explore in this coming section on Arrays.

4.1 Arrays and the Little Man Computer.

An array is a contiguous (one after the other) collection of mailboxes (memory locations). To get to some element in the array we need to be able to compute its address, given the base address and the offset of that element from the start of the array. This is the way that C like programming languages handle arrays.

If B is the base address and N is the offset of the element we are after in the array, then the address of that element is B + N. The first element has offset 0, and its address is B + 0. Providing we stick to the convention that an index is an offset then an index of R corresponds to element R + 1. The Little Man Computer cannot handle negative numbers so we are limited to positive offsets, which is perfectly good for getting started.

The instruction LDA is of the form 5xx. If B is the base address of our array, and N is the offset then an LDA that will load the data in the accumulator into the mailbox at address B + N can be computed as the following sum 500 + B + N. Similarly, for retrieving an element from a location with offset N from a base address B, and knowing that the instruction STA is of the form 3xx we can save a value in the accumulator into the mailbox at offset N from the base address by an instruction computed as 300 + B + N. Suppose we put our LDA instruction at an address, denoted symbolically, as readArr and we put our STA instruction at an address denoted symbolically by writeArr.

4.1.1 Writing an element to an array and reading an element from an array in the Little Man Computer.

We are going to explore arrays on the LMC using the following little challenge. How could we implement an LMC program that could read in an arbitrary number of elements into an array and then write out those elements in the order they were entered. We will assume that all the elements entered are positive and that the end of data entry is denoted by an input 000.

Rather than doing this all in one go we'll start by writing a simple program that, given a base address for an array, and an offset into the array will save a user entered value at that location. Then it will read the contents at that address and display the value retrieved.

This requires some careful planning and thinking. Lets think about the problems that we need to tackle.

- We craft a read instruction and save it at some defined location.
- To execute that instruction we have to jump (BRA) to that location.
- Having executed the instruction the instruction that will be run next is the one at the immediately following address.
- This instruction must take us to the instruction that we want to execute after the BRA to where the read instruction was saved.
    - We need a label to that instruction
    - And our instruction must BRA to the address associated with that label.
- A similar line of reasoning applies to reading an element at some specified offset in our array and then outputting its value.

The following piece of LMC assembler illustrates the technique to use:

Fig 4.1 Assembler for writing a value into an array and then retrieving and outputting that value.

```
        LDA wrCmd
        ADD base
        ADD offset
        STA write
        INP
        BRA write
retWr1  LDA rdCmd
        ADD base
        ADD offset
        STA read
        BRA read
retRd1  OUT
        HLT
offset  DAT 10
base    DAT 80
address DAT
write   DAT
        BRA retWr1
read    DAT
        BRA retRd1
rdCmd   DAT 500
wrCmd   DAT 300
```

```
00 LDA 21
01 ADD 14
02 ADD 13
03 STA 16
04 INP
05 BRA 16
06 LDA 20
07 ADD 14
08 ADD 13
09 STA 18
10 BRA 18
11 OUT
12 HLT
13 DAT 10
14 DAT 80
15 DAT 00
16 DAT 00
17 BRA 06
18 DAT 00
19 BRA 11
20 DAT 500
21 DAT 300
```

To really understand what is going on here you will need to step through the program an instruction at a time and really make sure you understand exactly what happens when the instruction is executed. Something that will help is to write down what the Little Man says in the speech bubble explaining what he is doing at each step of the way.

The base address of the array is given as 80

The offset is given as 10

This means that the destination for the user input is address 80 + 10 which is 90.

Before we get the input we need to construct a STA instruction that will store the user input at address 90, and then to save the resulting instruction in a defined location. In our case this is the address associated with the label write. We accomplish this via the instructions at adresses 00,01,02,03. The following screen snapshot shows the state of the Little Man Computer as we are about to execute the instruction at address 04.

Fig 4.2 State of the Little Man Computer after executing the command sequence 00,01,02,03.

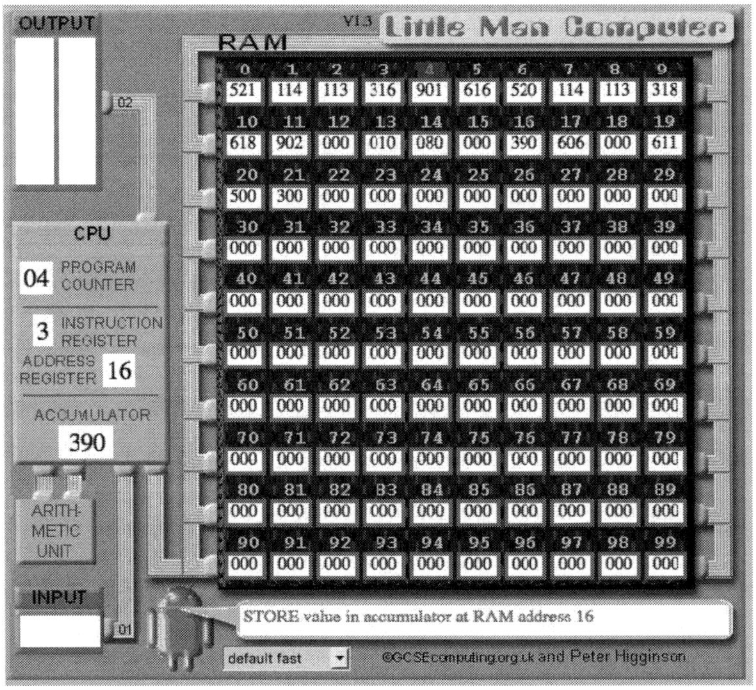

Lets examine the various parts of interest :

- The value in the accumulator is 390 the write instruction we computed.
- The write instruction itself is to be stored in a mailbox 16 - which is the mailbox associated with the label write.
- The instruction register and the address register contain the values 3 and 16 respectively which corresponds to the instruction STA 16 which we have just executed to store our computed write instruction at mailbox 16
- The program counter has a value 4 which is the address of the next instruction that we will execute.

We step on and are prompted to enter some input. Suppose we enter the value 33. This will result in a value of 33 being present in the accumulator and the program counter will now be 05. The instruction at 05 is BRA 16. Lets step on and execute that instruction. The snapshot of the Little Man Computer state at this point shows the following :

Fig 4.3. State of the Little Man Computer after executing the instruction at mailbox address 16.

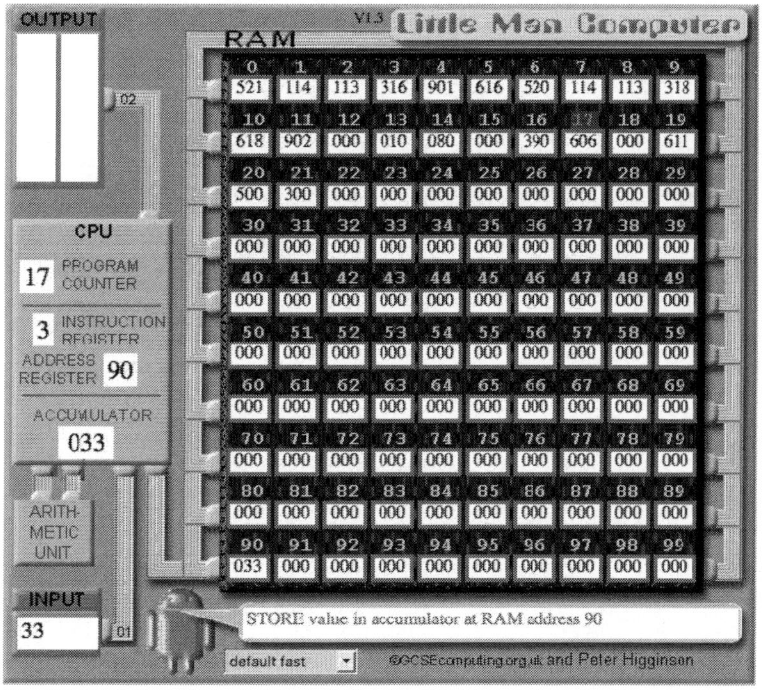

Looking at the state information we note that

- The next instruction to execute will be the one in mailbox 17 as per the value of the program counter. Also note the the value we entered (33 in this example) is now stored in the mailbox with address 90. Also note the contents of mailbox 17 which are 606 which is a branch to mailbox address 06 instruction, and note, by looking at the assembler that this is the address associated with the label retWr1 (a symbol I thought up meaning return after first write)

The instruction at mailbox address 16 is the first of three instructions to compute the instruction to read the data at the mailbox address 90 , which is the address computed by adding the offset to the base address. Stepping on and executing the instruction sequence 06,07,08,09 we end up with the BRA read (BRA 18) instruction at mailbox address 10. The state of the Little Man Computer is now.

Fig 4.4 State of Little Man Computer just before going to execute the instruction at mailbox 10. Which is BRA 18. If we look at the contents of mailbox 18 we see that it contains the value 590 which is LDA 90 i.e. load the contents of mailbox 90 into the accumulator.

Executing the instruction at mailbox 10 and then the instruction at mailbox 18 brings the Little Man Computer to the following state. We have just executed instruction 590 and the value in the accumulator is 33 which is the value held in mailbox 90. The program counter tells us that the address of the next instruction to execute is 19. Looking at the assembler we see that this is the instruction BRA retRd1, and that retRd1 is the symbol associated with instruction immediately after the BRA to the read instruction we have just recently executed. The instruction at retRd1 (address 11) is an OUT instruction ...

Pressing on and stepping through to the HLR instruction at mailbox address 12 results in the Little Man Computer reaching the following state.

Fig 4.5 State of the Little Man Computer after having retrieved and output a value from an array.

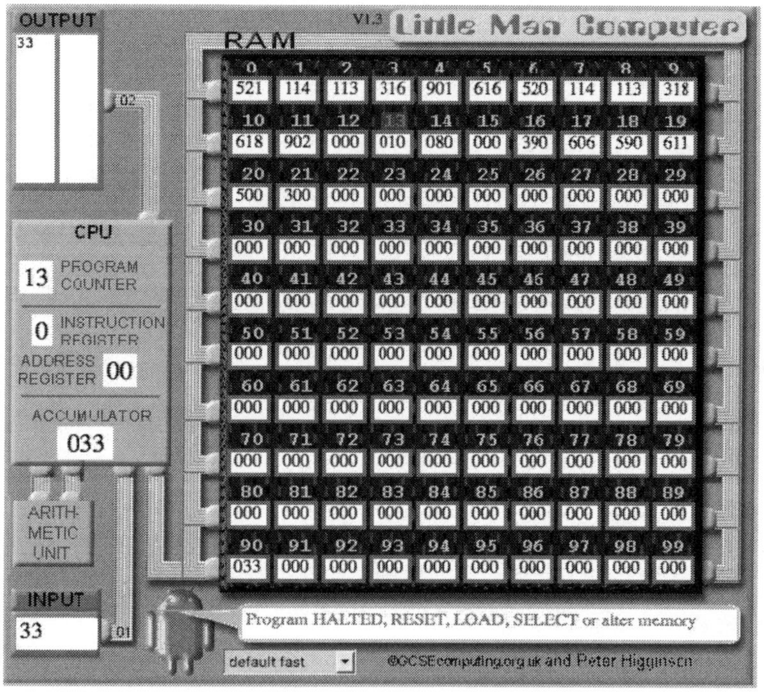

The value has been retrieved from the array and successfully output.

4.2 Writing a list of elements into an array.

The goal here is to write an LMC program that allows a user to load a list of positive numbers into an array. Entry terminates when the user enters a 000 value. This program is not a robust program , there is no checking for memory overflows, it is a starting program to demonstrate a basic pattern.

In pseudocode the program can be written as follows :

```
Set up base address for the array.
Set up an index variable
Initialise index to 0
WHILE input not equal to 0
      Read in next value
      Save it at address ( base + index )
      Increment index by one
ENDWHILE
HALT
```

The corresponding assembler uses the same techniques as in the previous section, and should be straightforward to follow.

Fig 4.6 Assembler code for program that writes input numbers into an array, starting at some initial offset (0 in this example) and keeps track of the offset at which the next number is to be placed.

```
          LDA wrCmd
          ADD base
          ADD offset
          STA write
next      INP
          BRZ done
          BRA write
retWr1    LDA offset
          ADD one
          STA offset
          LDA write
          ADD one
          STA write
          BRA next
done      HLT
offset    DAT 0
base      DAT 70
address   DAT
write     DAT
          BRA retWr1
one       DAT 1
wrCmd     DAT 300
```

```
00 LDA 21
01 ADD 16
02 ADD 15
03 STA 18
04 INP
05 BRZ 14
06 BRA 18
07 LDA 15
08 ADD 20
09 STA 15
10 LDA 18
11 ADD 20
12 STA 18
13 BRA 04
14 HLT
15 DAT 00
16 DAT 70
17 DAT 00
18 DAT 00
19 BRA 07
20 DAT 01
21 DAT 300
```

The thing to note in the assembler above is that we modify the write command to write to the next location by simply incrementing it via the sequence of instructions

LDA write
ADD one
STA write

The state of the Little Man Computer after entering the following sequence of numbers 1 2 3 4 5 6 0 is shown in Fig 4.7 .

Fig 4.7 State of Little Man Computer after entering an array of numbers

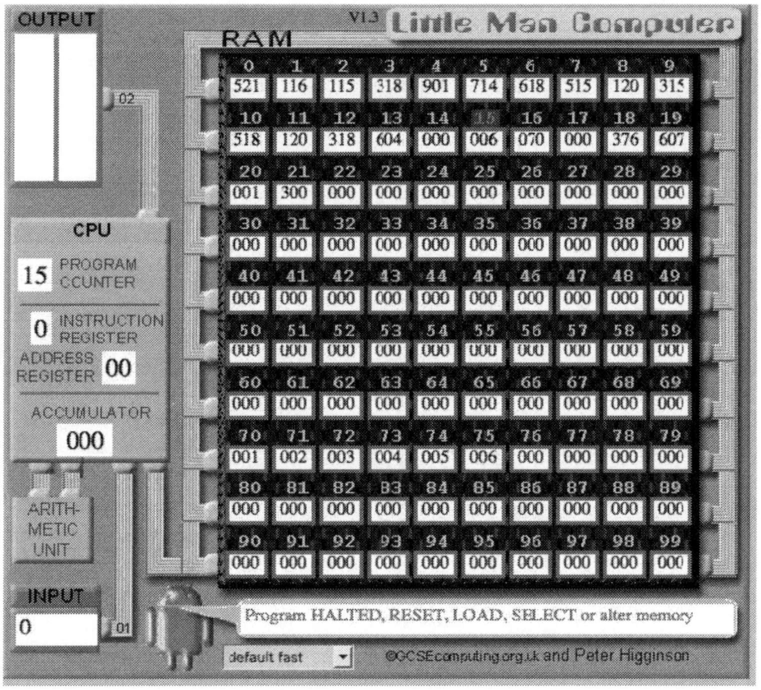

The numbers are present in mailboxes 70 to 76.

The code we have written can be simplified by placing the write label in the middle of the loop, thus avoiding a, possibly, rather clumsy branch.

The resulting (neater) code will now look like this :

Fig 4.8 Modified Code for entering an array of numbers.

```
        LDA wrCmd
        ADD base
        ADD offset
        STA write
next    INP
        BRZ done
write   DAT
        LDA offset
        ADD one
        STA offset
        LDA write
        ADD one
        STA write
        BRA next
done    HLT
offset  DAT 0
base    DAT 70
one     DAT 1
wrCmd   DAT 300
```

Writing clean assembler requires a lot of experience and practice. Once a program has been implemented and tested it can then be refined and optimised, as this example scenario has shown. Be warned, however, aggressive optimisation of assembler may result in code that is difficult to follow and maintain. Code that is fit for purpose and is not the most highly optimised, but, is readable and understandable may often be the best option.

4.3 Sorting an Array of Numbers

The goal here is to implement a program that will sort an array of numbers. The base address of the array and its size are known. Probably the simplest sorting algorithm is the bubble sort. It uses the simple strategy of traversing an array and comparing an element with its neighbour. If we are sorting in ascending order then if an element is larger than its immediate neighbour we swap them around and continue traversing the rest of the array. On each pass through the array the next highest element ends up in the correct position in the sorted array. If the array has size N, then after N passes it is sorted.

Supposing we have an array 10 5 4 6 3 7
On the first pass of the buble sort we will end up with 5 4 6 3 7 10
On the second pass of the bubble sort we will end up with 4 5 3 6 7 10
On the third pass of the bubble sort we will end up with 4 3 5 6 7 10
On the fourth pass of the bubble sort we will end up with 3 4 5 6 7 10
In the naive implementation the fifth and sixt passes would have no effect.

This simple sorting algorithm can be optimised by noting that after each pass the size of array we have to examine is smaller by one because the next highest element has found its correct position, and so on successive passes we are, in effect, sorting a smaller and smaller array. Another optimisation feature is that if we traverse the array without having to do a single swap then the array is sorted and the sort program is done.

The key operation is the swapping of two elements in the array. If the elements to be swapped are stored in addresses A and B, then we need a third address TMP, say to temporarily save one of the values.

The pseudocode for carrying out a swap operation is

```
Write contents of A to TMP
Write contents of B to A
Write contents of TMP to B
```

Lets start of by considering how we might implement the basic swap operation, where the elements to be swapped are at offsets OFFSET and OFFSET + 1 say. We need to construct read and write commands that do the following

Load data at BASE + OFFSET into the accumulator
Write value in accumulator to TMP
Load data at BASE + OFFSET + 1 into accumulator
Write value in accumulator to BASE + OFFSET
Load data at TMP into accumulator
Write value in accumulator to BASE + OFFSET + 1

The assembler in the Higginson sort example actually uses two temporary locations, buff1 and buff2.

In the bubble sort we are traversing the array sequentially from low order addresses to high order addresses. If we start of with basic instructions for loading an element at address X, say, into a temporary location buff1 and its neighbour , at address X + 1, into a temporary location buff2 then the value of an element and its neighbour can be compared by simply comparing the values in tmp1 and tmp2. If a swap is necessary then the value in buff1 is writted into mailbox X + 1 and the value in buff2 is written into mailbox X.

Consider the following small snippet of assembler based on the bubblesort example that is provided as part of the Higginson Little Man Computer distribution.

```
load1        DAT 580       // Initial load1 instruction
             STA buff1
load2        DAT 581       // Initial load2 instruction
             STA  buff2
```

Lets refer to the above block of instructions as “Write Current Pair of Elements to Temp Buffer”

The array starts at address 80.

buff1 and buff2 hold numbers, load1, load2, store1 and store2 hold instructions.

Fig 4.9 Snapshot of key variables and array contents at start of the bubble sort

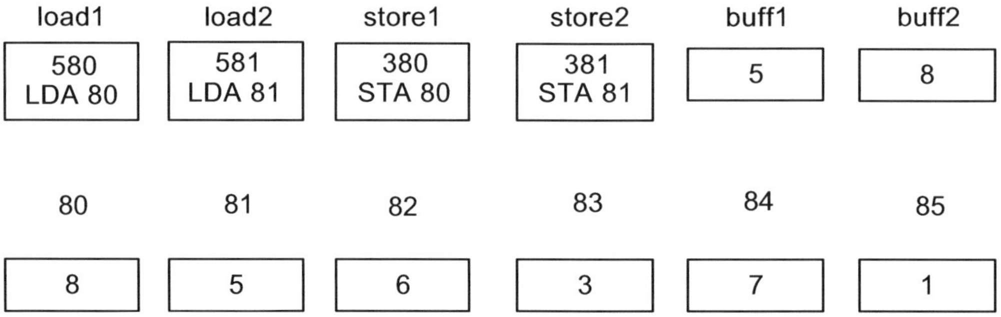


```
cmp         SUB buff1
            BRP nextPos
swap        LDA buff2
store1      DAT 380 // Initial value of store1 instruction
            LDA buff1
store2      DAT 381 // Initial value of store 2 instruction
```

Lets refer to the above block of instructions as “If first element greater than the second element swap elements in buffer”

With the array values given the end result after the swap will be as shown.

Fig 4.10 Snapshot of key variables and array contents of the bubble sort after the first swap

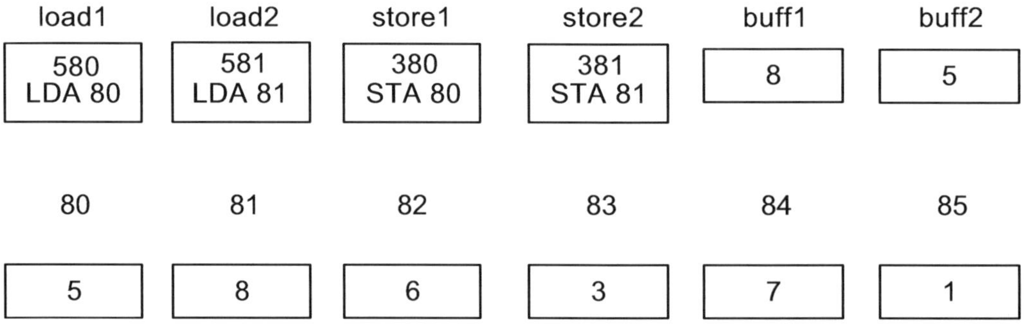

```
nextPos     LDA store1
            ADD one
            STA store1
            // LDA store2 - not necessary - because simply adding one to the instruction value in
            // the accumulator will give use the instruction we want
            ADD one
            STA store2
            LDA load1
            ADD one
            STA load1
            // LDA load2 - not necessary - for the same reason as above
            ADD one
            STA load2
```

Let's refer to the above block of code as "increment load and store instructions". With the array used in this example the result after executing this block of code will be as follows :

Fig 4.11 Snapshot of key variables and array contents of the bubble sort after incrementing the load and store instructions.

load1	load2	store1	store2	buff1	buff2
581 LDA 81	582 LDA 82	381 STA 81	382 STA 82	8	5

80	81	82	83	84	85
5	8	6	3	7	1

```
            // Code to check if sorting completed in which case
            // Jump to code to output the sorted list
            BRA load1 // Compare the pair of elements in the next position in the array
```

After a second iteration around the loop we will end up with the following state

Fig 4.11 Snapshot of key variables and array contents of the bubble sort after the second iteration of the bubble sort loop.

load1	load2	store1	store2	buff1	buff2
582 LDA 82	583 LDA 83	382 STA 82	383 STA 83	8	6

80	81	82	83	84	85
5	6	8	3	7	1

With this code that can traverse the data array , swapping adjacent elements as necessary , in place, we are now in a position to explore the overall logic of the bubble sort.

We store the STA and LDA instructions for reading and writing the first element of our array (the element whose offset is 0) in mailboxes (variables) sta0 and lda0, thus

```
sta0    DAT    380
lda0    DAT    580
```

We also have a variable listLen that holds the length of the list (array) of numbers, set up as follows

```
listLen         DAT    0
```

ListLen is set to the number of elements in the list as part of the array entry code.

Then, at the start of the loop that traverses the array performing swap operations as required we have instructions such as the following

```
sortPass        LDA    lda0
                STA    load1
                ADD    one
                STA    load 2
                LDA    sta0
                STA    store1
                ADD    one
                STA    store2
                // The above six instructions initialise load1, load2, store1 and store2 at the start of
                // a sorting pass through the array
```

We also need to track the number of times left to go round the sorting pass, and also a flag to indicate whether it was necessary to swap a pair of elements in a given sorting pass through the array. The initial value of this flag is set to zero. If a swap occurs the value of the flag is set to 1.

If at the end of a sorting pass the value of the flag is still 0 then the array is sorted and we can break out of the loop that is responsible for the next sorting pass.

```
LDA   listLen
SUB   one
STA   numItersLeft   // The number of steps along the array is one less than the
                     // number of elements in the array.
                     // This is because at each point we compare the current element
                     // with the next one ahead.
LDA   0
STA   swapFlag       // The swapFlag will be set to 1 if an actual swap takes place
                     // during a traversal of the array.
```

A complete bubblesort (based on Peter Higginson's example) is shown below, with comments.

Fig 4.11 Complete listing of the Bubblesort Program

```
                LDA lda0
                STA outputListItem
                LDA sta0
                STA storeListItem
                LDA zero
                STA listLen
inputLoop       INP
                BRZ resetLoop
storeListItem  DAT 380  //  If the program is reset the old value from the previous
                        // running of the program may not be 380
                        //  this is why the initialisation step at the start of the code
                        // is necessary.
                LDA storeListItem
                ADD one
                STA storeListItem
                LDA listLen
                ADD one
                STA listLen
                BRA inputLoop
sortPass        LDA lda1        // The bubblesort loop .. sets up the next pass through the array
                STA load1
                ADD one
                STA load2
                LDA sta1
                STA store1
                ADD onr
                STA store2
                LDA listLen
                SUB one
                STA numItersLeft
```

```
              LDA zero
              STA swapFlag  // initialise swapFlag to 0
              load1   DAT 580
              STA buffA
              load2   DAT 581
              STA buffB
cmp           SUB buffA
              BRP nextItem
swap          LDA buffB
store1        DAT 380       // These instructions are modified as the program runs to 3xx,
                            // Which is STA xx, where xx = 80 + offset
              LDA buffA
store2        DAT 381       // These instructions are modified as the program runs to 3yy,
                            // Which is STA yy, where yy = 81 + offset
              LDA one
              STA swapFlag //Set swapFlag to 1 as a swap operation has taken place.
// Next , increment the address parts of store1, store2, load1 and load2
nextItem      LDA store1
              ADD increment
              STA store1
              ADD increment
              STA store2
              LDA load1
              ADD increment
              STA load1
              ADD increment
              STA load2
// Decrement the loopCount
              LDA loopCount
              SUB increment
              STA loopCount
              BRZ isFinished  // Jump to doneSwap which fires up the next pass of the
                              // bubblesort loop , or, if the swapFlag is zero jumps out
                              // of the bubblesort loop
              BRA load1       // Move on to the next pair of elements in the list (array)
doneSwap      LDA isChange
              BRZ outputList
              bra sortPass
outputList    DAT 580       // This instruction is modified by the code when it runs
              OUT
              LDA outputList
              ADD increment
              STA outputList
              LDA listLen
              SUB one
              STA listLen
```

```
                BRZ done
                BRA outputList
done            HLT
zero            DAT 0
buffA   DAT 0
buffB   DAT 0
swapFlag        DAT 0
one             DAT 1
listLen DAT 0
numItersLeft    DAT 0
sta0            DAT 380
lda0            DAT 580
```

A high level pseudocode description of the bubble sort might look something like the following. It is assumed that the array is already present at a known starting address and that the number of elements in the array is known.

```
Define and initialise the variables array and arrayLen // which hold the start address of the array and
                                                      // the array length respectively
Define the swapFlag variable and initialise it to 1
Define the index variable i and initialise it to 0
Define the numIters variable and initialise it to arrayLen
Define the variables tmp1 and tmp2 // to hold values temporarily
WHILE (numIters > 0  AND  swapFlag is NOT equal to 1)
        initialise index variable to 0
        set swapFlag to 0
        WHILE ( i <  (arrayLen - 2))
                IF ( (arrayElement at address (array + i)) > (arrayElement at address (array + i + 1)))
                        save arrayElement at address (array + i) to tmp1
                        save arrayElement at address (array + i + 1) to tmp2
                        write value in tmp 2 to arrayElement at address (array + i)
                        write value in tmp 1 to arrayElement at address (array + i +1)
                        set swapFlag to 1
                ENDIF
                increment i
        ENDWHILE
        decrement numIters
ENDWHILE
```

Here is a translation of the pseudocode to Python. In Python array[i] refers to an object at offset i from the start of the array. The Python code is quite close to the pseudocode.

```
array = [4,7,2,11,33]
arrayLen = len(array)
numIters = arrayLen
i = 0
swapFlag = 1
tmp1 = 0
```

```
tmp2 = 0
while ((numIters > 0) & (swapFlag != 0)) :
    i = 0
    swapFlag = 0
    while (i < (arrayLen -2)) :
        if (array[i] > array[i + 1]) :
            tmp1 = array[i]
            tmp2 = array[i + 1]
            array[i] = tmp2
            array[i + 1] = tmp1
            swapFlag = 1
        i = i + 1
     numIters = numIters - 1
print(array)
```

I leave it is as an exercise for you to draw the corresponding flowhart.

4.4 Implementing a simple bootstrap program.

This is the last of the more advanced examples. In order for code to run on a computer it has to be, somehow, loaded into that computer. In the Little Man Computer simulator the code somehow "gets into the computer by magic". This is not the case in the real world.

The principles underlying the bootstrap program are very similar (though simplified) to the loader programs that start up a program under Windows or Linux, and to bootloader programs that come with many embedded systems applications.

The essential thing to be aware of, and we have already seen this in the bubblesort program is that an instruction can be considered as a piece of data.

The bootstrap program is written as follows

At mailbox 00 there is a permanent (i.e. it should not be overwritten) BRANCH (BRA) instruction to the start of the bootstrap program, which resides in the last mailbox locations. This program is permanent and should not be overwritten.

The bootstrap program reads in intructions as if they were data and stores them is successive mailbox addresses, starting at mailbox address 1. Then end of the program input is signified by an input value of 999. When the user inputs 999 the boostrap program jumps to location 01 and will then execute the program that has been entered.

To load (bootstrap) the times table program, using the assembler given earlier, we would need to start off with a working program , and because this includes labels and variables add an extra 'dummy' line of assembler e.g. BRA 001 to it and then assemble the code. If we then look at the mailbox entries in the Little Man Computer and take the entries from mailbox 1 till the end of the program we will end up with a sequence of numbers, and these are the numbers to enter when prompted to do so by the bootstrap program. Finally we will enter 999 to tell the bootstrap program that we have finishes entering code.

Lets try this out on a simple program that outputs a number, say, 7.

Here is the assembler :

```
        BRA 001
        LDA seven
        OUT
        HLT
seven   DAT 7
```

Assembling and running this program - it works, and we see that the machine code is
601,504, 902, 000, 007

So the numbers to enter when prompted to do so by the bootstrap program would be
504, 902, 000, 007, 999

The assembler for the bootstrap program is not particularly difficult. To locate it at the end of memory the assembler will need to have lots of DAT directives after the branch instruction BRA bootstrap in mailbox 000.

The actual assembler code is practically the same as the code for entering a whole lot of numbers into an array. The only extra part is a BRX startRun statement which is used to start the program running. Note, that startRun is the symbol associated with mailbox address 1.

The assembler for the bootstrap program would be something like the following :

```
      BRA bootstrap
startRun    DAT    000
            DAT
            DAT
// lots more DATS
            DAT
bootstrap   LDA    wrCmd
            ADD    base
            ADD    offset
            STA    write
next        INP
            STA    tmp
            SUB    endProg
            BRZ    startRun
            LDA    tmp
write       DAT    301
            LDA    write
            ADD    one
            STA    write
            BRA    next
offset      DAT    0
base        DAT    1
endProg     DAT    999
```

```
zero      DAT  0
one       DAT  1
index     DAT  1
tmp       DAT  0
wrCmd     DAT  300
```

If we run the bootstrap program and enter the instructions for the little program above the resulting state of the Little Man Computer will be as shown below.

Fig 4.12 State of the Little Man Computer after it has bootstrapped and executed a program.

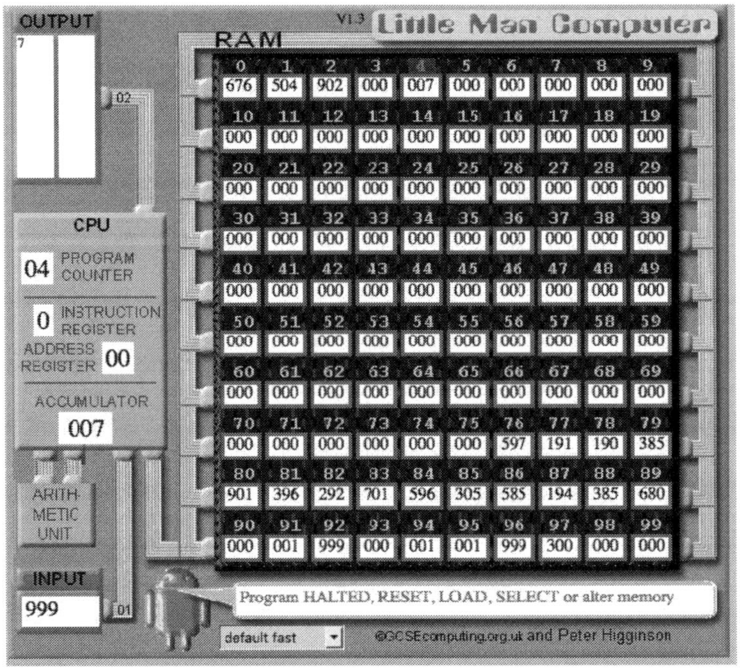

0	1	2	3	4	5	6	7	8	9
676	504	902	000	007	000	000	000	000	000
70	**71**	**72**	**73**	**74**	**75**	**76**	**77**	**78**	**79**
000	000	000	000	000	000	597	191	190	385
80	**81**	**82**	**83**	**84**	**85**	**86**	**87**	**88**	**89**
901	396	292	701	596	305	585	194	385	680
90	**91**	**92**	**93**	**94**	**95**	**96**	**97**	**98**	**99**
000	001	999	000	001	001	999	300	000	000

(Mailboxes 10–69 all contain 000.)

The points to note when looking at the contents of the little man computer are

- The bootstrap program itself which starts at (has an entry point) at mailbox address 76
- The instruction 676 (BRA 76) in mailbox 00 that branches to this entry point.
- The code of the program in mailboxes 01, 02, 03, 04.

You can experiment with entering longer programs, but it will involve quite a lot of patient data entry.

4.5 Concluding Remarks

Quite a lot of material has been covered in this book. It still astounds me how a simple architecture and a simple set of instructions can be used to produce some quite powerful computer programs. Amongst the "Best Computer Quotations" there is the following one, attributes to Albert Einstein.

Computers are incredibly fast, accurate and stupid. Humans beings are incredibly slow, inaccurate and brilliant. Together they are powerful beyond imagination. -- Albert Einstein, physicist and humanitarian (1879 - 1955)

So, where next ?

If you found this book fascinating then maybe you might be interested in exploring assembly language programming in greater depth e.g. by studying some follow up books to this one, such as

"PIC16 Assembly Language Programming from the Ground Up" by Andrew Eliasz

"ATMEL AVR Assembly Language Programming from the Ground Up" by Andrew Eliasz.

Wherever your interests take you - "Happy Programming".

References :

1. www.citidel.org/bitstream/10117/117/6/LMMS.pdf - LMMS an 8 bit microcode simulator
2. https://helios.hud.ac.uk/scomhro/Papers/JERIC/jeric.ps - The Postroom Computer
3. http://ocw.covenantuniversity.edu.ng/faculty/stuart-madnick/ - Faculty Profile entry for Stuart Madnick - Includes some lovely biographical details.
4. The Architecture of Computer Hardware, Systems Software, and Networking - An Information Technology Approach - 5Ed, by Irv Englander , pub Wiley 2014
5. Peter Higginson's Little Man Computer Simulator - http://peterhigginson.co.uk/LMC/
6. https://www.edrawsoft.com/flowchart-examples.php
7. Corrado; B. and Jacopini, G. (May 1966). “Flow Diagrams, Turing Machines and Languages with Only Two Formation Rules”. Communications of the ACM 9 (5): 366–371.
8. PDL Standard http://users.csc.calpoly.edu/~jdalbey/SWE/pdl_std.html
9. Best Computer Quotations http://www.linfo.org/q_computer.html

APPENDIX A

Practice Exam Questions on Very Simple Programs and How the Little Man Computer Works

Beginning students are not, generally, expected to implement the more complicated LMC programs that have been discussed here. Students on more advanced courses (e.g. beginning undergraduate courses) are, however, expected to be able to implement not only basic (e.g. add two numbers) but more advanced (e.g. sort the elements in an array of numbers) programs.

Exercises in implementing programs are given at the end of Chapters 3 and 4.

The "exam type" questions included here are more in the style of written answers to questions about how the LMC works. They can be thought of as being helpful when revising and preparing to answer these kinds of LMC exam questions. To answer some of the questions you may need to review various topics in your computer science course that are not covered in detail here.

1. Sketch out a diagram of the Little Man Computer clearly labeling the various components. For each component give a brief description of its function and purpose.

2. Real processors and computer systems use buses to move data around. How are such buses modeled in the Little Man Computer ?

3. Describe carefully the steps taken by the Little Man when executing an INPUT instruction.

4. Explain the characteristic features of a von Neuman computer architecture. Does the Little Man Computer architecture exhibit the characteristics of a von Neuman computer architecture or not ?

   Carefully explain your reasoning.

5. Describe the instruction cycle of a typical computer and use the Little Man Computer model to illustrate this cycle in action.

APPENDIX B. The PDL Standard Constructs [8]

Here we describe / illustrate the Pseudocode Language constructs given in the PDL Standard. Note that numbering and subnumbering is used to label statements and substatements, and that indentation is also used to make the code easier to follow, especially when there a nested loops or nested selections.

- Computation/Assignment
  - Compute var1 as the sum of x and y
  - Assign the value of an expression to var2
  - Increment counter1
- Input/Output
  - Input: Get var1, var2, ...
  - Output: Display var1, var2, ...
- Selection
  - Single-Selection IF

1. IF condition THEN (IF condition is true, then do subordinate statement 1, etc. If condition is false, then skip statements)
    1.1 statement 1
    1.2 further statements etc.

- Double-Selection IF - ELSE

2. IF condition THEN (IF condition is true, then do subordinate statement 1, etc. If condition is false, then skip statements and execute statements under ELSE)
    2.1 statement 1
    2.2 other statements

3. ELSE (else if condition is not true, then do subordinate statement 2, etc.)
    3.1 statement 2
    3.2 other statements

- SWITCH expression TO (multiple choices based on the value returned when the expression is evaluated)
    4.1 case 1: perform action1
    4.2 case 2: perform action2
    4.3 etc.
    4.4 default: actionx

- Repetition
    - WHILE loop - tests a condition at the start of each iteration of the while loop. (while the condition remains true, then do subordinate statements. Terminate the while loop when the condition evaluates to false. The condition is evaluated each time around the loop. A WHILE loop may thus execute the subordinate statements in the body 0 or more times, because if the condition evaluated to false when the loop is entered, the body of the loop will never be executed)
        5. WHILE condition
        5.1 statement 1
        5.2 other statements.

- DO – WHILE structure (this is like WHILE, except that the test condition is evaluated at the end of the loop. A DO - WHILE loop will execute the subordinate statements in the body of the loop structure at least once.)
    6. DO
        6.1 statement 1
        6.2 other statements
    7. WHILE condition

- FOR structure (this can be thought of as a specialisation of the WHILE loop in which the statements in the body of the loop are executed a specified number of time).

    8. FOR bounds on repetition
        8.1 statement 1
        8.2 other statements.

APPENDIX 2. Pseudocode rules used in the examples in this book.

There are, as has been mentioned ,variations on pseudocode. In a formal real world situation you may be asked to following one convention (set of pseudocode rules) as opposed to another. In this book we will use the following set of rules.

Rule 1. Write only one statement per line

- Each statement in the pseudocode should express just one action for the computer to perform.

Rule 2. The following keywords are used **READ, WRITE, IF, ELSE, ENDIF, WHILE, ENDWHILE , DO** (used in the DO - WHILE construct).

Rule 3. An initial keyword in a statement will be written in uppercase e.g. READ number

Rule 4. The hierarchy of statements in a pseudocode description of a program will be shown by the use of indentation e.g.

```
IF amount greater than 200
        deduction = amount * deductionRate
ELSE
        deduction = 0
ENDIF
```

The indentation rules for the various pseudocode code constructs of sequence, selection and repetition (looping) are :

SEQUENCE: keep statements that are “stacked” in a sequence all with the same level of indentation. You can think of indentation as helping to identify blocks of code inside other blocks of code.

SELECTION: indent the statements that fall inside the selection structure, but not the keywords that form the selection indent

REPETITION: indent the statements that fall inside the loop, but not the keywords that form the loop.

Rule 5. End multiline structures correctly e.g.

- An IF should have a matching ENDIF at the same level of indentation as the matching IF
- A WHILE should have a matching ENDWHILE at the same level of indentation as the matching WHILE

Rule 6. Keep the pseudocode statements independent from any particular programming language such as e.g. don’t write pseudocode using e.g. BASIC or PYTHON syntax.

APPENDIX 3 Pseudocode and Flowcharts - Pros (Advantages) and Cons (Disadvantages)

- Pseudocode Disadvantages
  - Pseudocode is not particularly visual
  - There is no widely accepted standard for writing pseudocode.
    - There are wide variations between differeng companies and organisations.
  - Pseudocode Advantages
    - Pseudocode can be created readily using a text editor or word processor.
    - Modifying pseudocode at the textual level is relatively quick and easy.
    - Structured concepts are straightforward to represent and implement using pseudocode.
- Flowchart Disadvantages
  - Flowcharts are relatively difficult to modify.
    - Modifying fairly complex diagrams using drawing tools can be a time consuming and laborious process.
    - Using flowcharts requires diagramming software that can be used to draw these flowcharts.
    - Flowcharts do not provide explicit support for structured design elements e.g.
      - The same decision element (diamond) is used in the implementation of IF - ELSE and WHILE loops.
- Flowchart Advantages
  - Symbols and their meanings are standardised.
  - Provide a visual representation of a program or algorithm, however,
    - For complex algorithms flowcharts can be difficult to follow.

21978729R00049

Printed in Great Britain
by Amazon